PRAISE FOR *B2B CONTENT MARKE*

"Cuts through the marketing noise with a framework that reminds us what we forget in our rush to automate everything: You can't have ROI without the human connection."
Ann Handley, *Wall Street Journal* best-selling author of *Everybody Writes*, Chief Content Officer at Marketing Profs, keynote speaker, and social media influencer

"Devin Bramhall is one of the brightest minds in marketing. Her experience leading one of the most respected content marketing agencies shows in every insight she shares—always tactical, always thoughtful, and always with an edge of wit that makes you pay closer attention. If you're looking for a smarter way to think about content and the business of marketing, you're in the best possible hands."
Amanda Natividad, VP Marketing, SparkToro

"There's the way people tell you that marketing works, and then there's the way it actually works—the kind of experience you can only get from a decade-plus of taking your lumps ... or by listening to Devin Bramhall. I can't wait to send this to everyone on my team."
Sean Blanda, Owner, Gate Check Studios

"This is a marketing truth-teller at her best, and it's a good thing too: B2B marketers desperately need to evolve."
Jay Acunzo, author of *Break the Wheel: Question Best Practices, Hone Your Intuition, and Do Your Best Work*

"Devin Bramhall's authentic voice and originality of thought come through the written words like you're sitting across from a friend, if your friend happened to be one of the sharpest marketing minds you've ever met. Devin doesn't just challenge conventional wisdom; she ignores it entirely when it doesn't serve her systems-level thinking."
Allison Byers, Founder and CEO at Scroobious, angel investor, and advisor

B2B Content Marketing Strategy

*A Media-First Framework
That Accelerates Growth*

Devin Bramhall

KoganPage

First published in Great Britain and the United States in 2026 by Kogan Page Limited

Kogan Page
Kogan Page Ltd, 2nd Floor, 45 Gee Street, London EC1V 3RS, United Kingdom
Kogan Page Inc, 8 W 38th Street, Suite 902, New York, NY 10018, USA
www.koganpage.com

EU Representative (GPSR)
Authorised Rep Compliance Ltd, Ground Floor, 71 Baggot Street Lower, Dublin D02 P593, Ireland
www.arccompliance.com

Kogan Page books are printed on paper from sustainable forests.

ISBNs
Hardback   978 1 3986 2251 7
Paperback   978 1 3986 2250 0
Ebook   978 1 3986 2252 4

British Library Cataloguing-in-Publication Data
A CIP record for this book is available from the British Library.

Library of Congress Control Number
2025031488

Typeset by Integra Software Services, Pondicherry
Printed and bound by CPI Group (UK) Ltd, Croydon CR0 4YY

For Arestia and Jacqueline, who made my dreams come true.

CONTENTS

FOREWORD

"Devin is a Phoenix."

I considered having that be all I wrote. The world's first four-word foreword. It would be more than effective as an introduction to this book and to Devin. For whatever lens you choose to peer through and see Devin—whether you look back or ahead, whether you look professionally or personally—it is Devin as a Phoenix that will ring true.

We didn't meet under the best circumstances. I'd just accepted an offer to be the Chief Growth Officer of a popular startup and the CEO introduced me to her as my new Director of Content.

Devin was a direct report *assigned to me*. And I could see from Devin's expression that she was experiencing an equivalent level of surprise at being assigned a new boss.

Don't hire people for your team leaders; let your team leaders build their teams. That is a belief I've held throughout my career, one I've shared with the countless executives I've advised... unless you're hiring Devin.

When she entered the office and walked up to a group of us standing outside a conference room, she was a giant, fast-paced, confident burst of energy, which she maintained as we both learned that day about a marketing initiative and partnership she was to take over. The company had already invested significant time and budget on the project and it was in need of a strategic plan.

On the same day I met Devin, she was assigned direct reports she didn't hire, a boss she'd never met, and a substantial project already in motion that she had to bridle and steer in the direction of positive outcomes.

She didn't miss a beat as her surprised expression quickly snapped back into that energetic smile. Like the best freestyle emcees of hip hop's golden era, Devin took it all in and created a gameplan that was beautiful and lethally efficient and productive in both structure and form.

In the 18 months we worked together, she engineered an authentic evolution of the company's go-to-market messaging, supported a critical fundraise with a powerful narrative, and left the company significantly stronger, more capable, more informed, and more ready for the years that followed.

But she didn't conjure a plan out of thin air. Devin methodically broke down the project, assessed the team, and listened deeply before she acted. This wasn't magic—it was method. And it's exactly the kind of method she's sharing in these pages.

Since then, I've seen Devin transform both thriving and struggling initiatives into success stories. She has faced high-stakes challenges, both professionally and personally, and emerged stronger every time. Her strength lies in her ability to deliver exceptional work under any circumstances.

No matter where she starts, no matter the obstacles, she rises again and again. She is incredibly self-aware, intensely curious, and remarkably brave. This book is going to highlight for you the importance of finding those three within yourself. For there are no valuable or successful frameworks to be applied if you don't start with honest self-awareness, a commitment to curiosity, and a willingness to be brave.

Devin doesn't want you to be like her. She wants to unleash the best of you while being curious and brave in pursuit of your charge.

Eighty-five percent of us believe we're self-aware, but research shows only 10–15 percent of us actually are. Devin's story and this book are here to help you close that gap—to show you how to rise again and again, not by chance, but by choice.

Go be a Phoenix.

Suneet Bhatt
Recovering Executive, Executive Coach,
Lecturer on Purpose, EOS Implementor

ACKNOWLEDGMENTS

There's no way I will be able to thank everyone who deserves it in the 25 minutes I have left before I deliver the final manuscript. It's my own doing, really. It turns out that being an excellent writer and knowing what I want to say is not enough to get me to finish a book on time. Or by the many extensions they gave me after. It is the extreme pressure of having a finite number of minutes that got me to the finish line. Which is why many of you who deserve it won't be listed here. So here is what I have to say to you: I wouldn't be me without you, and I love that most of all.

Mom, dad, Ali, you are responsible for all the best parts of me, and I love you so much. Thank you for loving and supporting me so completely that even I couldn't argue you out of it.

Liz and Lauren, my ride or dies and co-wine and fries. You showed me how to lead with strength through my heart and sharpened my skills by the example you set in your own lives. Here's to Mary Beth and Susie Lou, who said F you to Jean Claude and the patriarchy. You can't put baby in the corner but, as we discovered, she fits surprisingly well in a bag sometimes.

Emily Martin, who gave me friendship and a family when I really needed both. The most loyal devil's angel I've ever met. Let's never change and wear sweatsuits to happy hour 4EVA. Where's the pewl?

Pam and Karen: Meeting you and having you in my life has been one of the greatest gifts of my life. I love you both so much and feel grateful for you every day. Thank you for your love, laughs, and for knowing a part of me that no one else does.

Chad O'Connor, Chris Roland, and the Father, the Son, and the Holy Spirit.

Ashley Faus, I know you hate when I get all mushy but you've shown up in my life—on purpose—in really meaningful and impactful ways. You've nudged me, even when I resisted. You've sparred with me and made me better. And you used your halo to elevate me when you didn't have to. You are a great friend.

Alex Birkett: Thank you for seeing me through cancer and caring about the book—and me.

Donna: You reached out and offered me something I've always wanted, and I will never forget that. Bobbi-Lee, gosh, I'm grateful for your patience, kindness, support—everything. Also, I'm really, really sorry for the rush at the end!

Mike King: For doing something different and reminding me how exciting our work can be if we dream and do big.

Brian Carr. Thank you for believing in me way back before there was any proof it was worth it. And Mark O'Toole for being the first to say yes to the Master Slam and supporting me ever since.

And lastly, but only for dramatic effect, thank you Diana Humphrey for giving me my first job and lovingly holding me to high standards. You set me up to be exceptional, and I am, and will always be grateful to you for that.

Introduction

WHAT IS CONTENT?

The problem with the whole "content is king" narrative is its inherent fragility.

Kings can be conquered.
Kings die.

Empires crumble from within.
"We need content," my former favorite phrase, now makes my hair stand on end.

"Do you?" I reply,
the ghost of King Content haunting my present-day good sense.
I'm not saying content is dead (though it certainly isn't king).

But still, it's worth considering:

What do you need content for?

Because,
in the end, do you want to be the hoodwinked "King of Content"
or the child who sees
you're just a naked man prancing down the street.

You know how the simplest questions can leave you totally stumped?

It happened to me a few years ago when I was sitting at the bar of some suburban restaurant outside Boston with my dad. I was telling him about a client I was working with as part of my fractional CMO consulting. After listening patiently, he asked me a very simple question:

"What is content marketing?"

Normally, content marketers love a good "what is" question. We live for them. They're our bread and butter, our chance to explain our value and showcase our expertise. But when trying to explain it to someone who isn't in the industry, I struggled.

After fumbling for a minute, I grabbed a napkin and a pen and drew my answer by showing how content marketing fits within marketing generally.

I explained that marketing generally falls into two buckets—organic and paid—and gave examples of tactics to illustrate the difference, explaining how content marketing was about creating valuable information that attracts an audience rather than interrupting them with traditional advertising.

My dad looked at me for a second, then said, "So it's just marketing, then. You DO marketing."

I laughed. He wasn't wrong.

The conversation stuck with me and at first, I couldn't figure out why. Then one day it hit me over the head, and I realized I had a problem.

It's the same problem a lot of us in the marketing industry have. We're so myopically focused on how content marketing "should" be

FIGURE 0.1 What is Marketing?

What is Marketing?

Organic	Paid
Attract people to you	Have people delivered
• Blogs and social • PR • Events • Media (audio and video) • Newsletters	• Paid search and social • Display ads • Out-of-home • Print buying lists

done and fretting about how technological and macroeconomic changes impact what we do that we've kind of lost the plot.

We obsess over definitions of quality content, customer journey maps, the "right" ways to measure impact. We talk about it on LinkedIn, we give talks about it at conferences, we write endless articles dissecting every platform update and algorithm change. And we create entire businesses around helping companies do marketing. I built one of the most renowned and respected content marketing agencies in B2B SaaS with the earnest (and naïve) mission of "making the internet a more helpful place."

And we do all this, in part, because we want to know everything about the marketing tools, online platforms, norms, and trends so we can "do marketing" better—for our companies, our careers, and our own curiosity. All good things!

The problem, though, is that in our pursuit of "doing marketing" better, we've forgotten something important:

Marketing isn't always the best solution to growth.

And by thinking about growing businesses solely through the lens of "doing marketing," you automatically limit yourself to the tools, processes, playbooks, and plans that everyone else is using to achieve the same shortlist of outcomes.

Which means that when you say you're creating a marketing "strategy," you're just executing the same plan as everyone else. And guess what?

That's not strategy.

While running the content marketing agency, I remember hearing the same two requests on every sales call. "We need marketing!" and "It's time for marketing!"

My response: "Why?"

What I meant by that was, "What outcomes are you looking for?" and I asked it on purpose. Serving the B2B SaaS industry, I spoke to a lot of startup founders and CEOs who had no marketing experience and were often reluctantly engaging in content marketing at the behest of investors, friends, or the reality that their product would not, in fact, sell itself. So, their answer revealed to me whether they were thinking strategically about growing their company or checking a box that they may or may not believe in checking off.

The difference matters a lot, because I believe content marketers—myself included for a while—are also checking the content marketing box under a similar zombie-like trance and that's a far bigger contributor to the plateau in content's impact on growth than any of the AI or algorithm developments we fret so much about.

(Like I said, we've lost the plot.)

It's time to get off the hamster wheel and onto a less prescriptive path where we can all create truly unique growth journeys.

This book isn't about "doing marketing" better. It's about building a strategic approach that includes leveraging content—along with other things like your company's unique advantages—to drive business growth.

I know what you're thinking and you're absolutely right:

Your CEO isn't ready for this at all. And your CFO? They're going to hate the lack of certainty in this approach. I get it! They have their own stakeholders they are accountable to and confounding norms they must deal with. Being a CEO forever changed my perspective on marketing, because I finally understood why some of my ideas had been turned down in the past. It also revealed the limitations I'd unknowingly placed on my own content-based growth strategy.

When I began consulting a few years later, I was able to put this new dual perspective to use and very quickly I started having more fun and making companies a lot more money, faster, often without doing much marketing at all.

So instead of rehashing the same playbooks and tactics everyone else is using, I'm going to suggest a framework for revealing strategic advantages you can leverage to achieve growth outcomes. The kind of advantage that doesn't disappear when algorithms change or platforms fall out of favor.

After all, effective content strategy isn't about doing the "right" things; it's about doing things that help your business and customers achieve their desired growth outcomes while creating an unfair advantage over competition using the resources available to you and the circumstances in which you are operating.

Which is exactly how content marketing itself came to be and prevailed for a period of time. And it's worth revisiting quickly how we got here, because it helps reveal how current challenges are really the next big opportunity for content marketers to get back to higher ROI, if they're willing to throw away their old maps and start drawing new ones.

How Venture Funding Broke B2B Marketing

Here's the thing: Those content marketing playbooks you covet, they evolved out of the B2B SaaS boom in the early aughts and honestly, they don't even work that well.

Think about it: One of the biggest blockers content marketers face is getting the buy-in, budget, and reasonable time to execute these playbooks. And while we point fingers at the C-suite and investors, for some reason we haven't considered whether a playbook that most leaders don't want to invest in is strategic in the first place.

I'm not saying B2B executives generally make good decisions around marketing. In my experience working with hundreds of B2B companies, the vast majority don't. But that's exactly why content marketing playbooks that don't account for common obstacles are not only indefensible approaches to growth, they're also illogical.

How did we get here?

You could trace it back to the early mid-aughts when the Community Management role met the recently reformed SEO, which had experienced a Gandalf-style rebirth, trading its black hat for white to usher in an entirely new form of marketing in the digital age.

If you went that route, you might even include HubSpot, which certainly didn't invent Content Marketing but was perhaps the most successful at leveraging it. They swooped in and made playbooks and named things and all of us were like, "Yay!" and proceeded to execute them like they were born out of the Big Bang.

The brilliance of HubSpot's quick rise to Mother of Inbound Marketing isn't the playbooks themselves. Rather, it's the growth strategy they deployed. They leveraged a moment in time to create an "unfair" advantage by executing a long-term brand and community-building strategy that was designed to secure more than just the next quarter's sales; it would position them as the perceived mother of modern digital marketing, which served one of the fastest-growing industries—B2B SaaS.

But if you want to understand why HubSpot's approach worked, you'd zoom out just a little more to understand the economic conditions that facilitated the relationship between venture capital and B2B marketing.

As John-Henry Scherck, CEO of the B2B content and SEO agency Growth Plays, explains:

> When rates fell to near zero in December 2008, traditional yield plays—bonds, dividend stocks, even cash—lost their appeal. At the same time, tech and cloud infrastructure were gaining momentum, and venture capital positioned itself as the gateway to the next era of growth.
>
> Limited Partners, desperate for returns, started treating venture like a core strategy rather than a high-risk outlier. In the years that followed, a handful of firms delivered extraordinary wins, but most didn't. By the time COVID hit and rates dropped even further, the flywheel had gone into overdrive: too much capital chasing too few real opportunities. The promise of venture became less about outsized returns and more about everyone believing they'd be the exception.
>
> The result wasn't an innovation renaissance—it was homogeneity and mediocrity at scale. And we content marketers used our trusty playbooks to help these companies to trudge along a little longer. This

wasn't necessarily a bad thing, it just proliferated a single approach to growth that is inherently suboptimal for the VC-backed companies it primarily served.

Think about it: VC-backed companies need exponential growth on compressed timelines, which puts pressure on content marketers to demonstrate rapid growth. I saw this firsthand while running a content marketing agency. On calls with prospective customers, I heard the same requests over and over: Launch a search-driven content marketing initiative to reduce their reliance on paid spend; scale existing content marketing 10x to power hyper growth mode.

This focus on raw numbers rather than effectiveness manifested in:

- prioritizing lead quantity over quality
- creating content for algorithms rather than people
- measuring activity instead of impact

The venture-backed growth model influenced marketing budgets, timelines, and tactics that became standard practice for all B2B companies. It also led to the prioritization of metrics that matter to investors rather than metrics that build enduring businesses or serve customers.

The consequences extend even further:

- Only 17 percent of venture-backed B2B companies achieved successful exits between 2020 and 2024, and just 11 percent of all B2B acquisitions returned more than 3x on invested capital.[1]
- Average customer acquisition costs for B2B SaaS companies increased 70 percent between 2018 and 2023, while conversion rates declined by 30 percent.[2]

Yet tech startups continue to take venture funding and hire content marketers who deploy their playbooks. When they inevitably miss targets or they hit targets but down-funnel numbers are lower than expected or we just breathe wrong, the predictable skepticism ensues on the part of CEOs and CFOs who have to represent these results to their investors and then the CTO or Head of Product chimes in saying we should have focused on the product the whole time.

How's Everybody Doing?

Now might be a good time to remind those of you working in B2B SaaS that not every B2B company follows the venture-backed model. Bootstrapped companies, for example, have more control over how fast they grow, which opens the door to more marketing approaches than venture-backed businesses and enables them to invest in assets and relationships that compound over time. Just saying!

The SEO Content Playbook: From Innovation to Saturation

The content marketing revolution initially promised an elegant solution to growth challenges: Create helpful content, optimize it for search, and generate a perpetual stream of organic traffic converting into leads and customers.

This approach generated compounding returns for early adopters like HubSpot, Intercom, and Buffer that built massive audiences through educational content while simultaneously establishing category dominance.

The playbook was clear:

1 Identify high-volume keywords relevant to your solution.
2 Create comprehensive content addressing those search queries.
3 Optimize for search engines using proven technical practices.
4 Convert traffic into leads through strategic calls-to-action.
5 Nurture those leads toward purchase.

Venture capitalists loved this model because it was:

- scalable (more content = more traffic)
- measurable (traffic, rankings, conversions)
- predictable (follow the formula, get results)

But what happens when everyone follows the same playbook?

Amanda Natividad, VP of Marketing at SparkToro and the originator of "zero-click content," describes the current state: "In a time when content saturation is higher than ever before and when nearly 60 percent of all Google searches end without a click, you need to be value-driven. You need to continually win over your audience's attention. And you do this by posting platform-native content to social media. By optimizing for your content to get seen, not clicked."

These playbooks haven't failed because they were fundamentally flawed—they've declined because their effectiveness relied on specific market conditions that no longer exist:

1 Relative content scarcity: Early content marketers faced less competition and could establish authority more easily.

2 Trust in branded content: Audiences were more receptive to company-created content before experiencing repeated disappointment.

3 Lower acquisition costs: Channels were less saturated, allowing for more cost-effective customer acquisition.

4 Simpler attribution: Customer journeys were more straightforward and easier to track.

The problem is that B2B marketers continue following these playbooks even as the conditions that made them effective have fundamentally changed.

The C-Suite Problem

Let's start with what we already know: The biggest challenge for marketing leaders is convincing the people with money and decision-making power to let them do marketing and do it "right" (i.e. in a way that makes meaningful impact on company growth).

According to the CMO Council, 40 percent of CMOs cite proving ROI and attribution as their top challenge,[3] while research from McKinsey reveals a fundamental disconnect: "About 50 percent of our CEO respondents said they feel comfortable with modern marketing. However, 66 percent of the CMOs we surveyed said their CEOs were not comfortable with modern marketing."[4]

It's not just the CEO saying no.

In a 2019 survey of CFOs, McKinsey showed just 50 percent believe marketing is successful at driving growth.[5] Anecdotally, lack of marketing expertise seems to be the common factor among most marketing naysayers, and this same study also points in that direction, showing that only 3 percent of board members they surveyed have a marketing background. "Everyone [on the board] has an opinion about marketing," said one former apparel CEO, "but there is very little expertise."[6]

When executives don't understand marketing's contribution, the result is perpetual insecurity and diminishing investment. This explains why 42.2 percent of marketers say their marketing is underfunded,[7] creating a vicious cycle of underperformance and underinvestment.

The second biggest challenge marketers face, therefore, is maintaining that buy-in so they can execute long enough and secure the appropriate budget to show results.

It takes bravery to publicly fail and learn, not just as a marketer but as a brand, and many executives refuse to go there. That's why so many brands continue to do "what's always been done before"; they know what to expect and how to mitigate risk. Thus, a content marketer's job is less about creativity, campaigns, and experiments and more about mastering internal politics.

What Is Content Marketing?

Going back to my dad's original question, I'd answer it differently now:

Content marketing is a strategic growth plan that capitalizes on unique advantages, available resources, and current circumstances to make maximum impact on outcomes using minimal effort.

It is also NOT designed to be sustained forever, because things change. It's designed to get you to the next right place.

The Path Forward: Redefining B2B Marketing Strategy

The next generation of B2B content marketing strategy isn't about abandoning everything that came before. It's about building on proven foundations by challenging the assumptions that have shaped B2B marketing for the past decade so we can adapt to the new realities of how buyers make decisions and how companies create sustainable growth.

It's a good time to reassess how B2B content marketing creates value for both customers and companies in today's environment.

Interestingly, many of these shifts represent a return to marketing fundamentals that got lost in the race for scalable, measurable tactics:

- Channels → environments: Moving from channel-centric thinking to creating environments where your audience naturally engages.

- Metrics → meaning: Balancing short-term performance metrics with long-term brand and relationship building.

- Content → community: Shifting from one-way content broadcasting to facilitated community connection.

- Scale → specificity: Reaching the people whom you can logically impact rather than creating a superficial fan base.

- Automation → authenticity: Leveraging technology to enable human connection and strategic thinking rather than just "doing more."

The next generation of B2B marketing strategy isn't about abandoning everything that came before. It's about adapting our foundations to the new realities of how humans make decisions, how technology shows up in our lives, and the opportunities therein for you to invent new ways to grow companies.

I'm Not Here to Show You *the* Way I'm Here to Show You *a* Way

This book, my advice, and experiences certainly don't represent the totality of what is possible in the world, so I've included stories, strategies, and ideas of the brilliant marketers who have inspired me along the way.

I know some of this may sound vague, pie in the sky conceptual, but this is what real strategic thinking looks like! It doesn't come from prescribed playbooks. It comes from learning how to think for yourself. In fact, the premise of the strategy I present in this book is that there is no predefined "way," and that is your second greatest advantage.

Your number one advantage? That's you. Time to show the world what you've got.

Notes

1   Svb.com (2024) State of the Markets Report H1 2024, Silicon Valley Bank, www.svb.com/trends-insights/reports/state-of-the-markets-report/h1-2024/ (archived at https://perma.cc/BV84-6JAD)

2   OpenView (2023) OpenView's 2023 SaaS Benchmarks is here! https://openviewpartners.com/2023-saas-benchmarks-report/ (archived at https://perma.cc/FS7M-U2WK)

3   Managing Marketing Technology, Growth, and Sustainability (2024) https://cmosurvey.org/wp-content/uploads/2024/04/The_CMO_Survey-Highlights-and-Insights-Report-Spring_2024.pdf (archived at https://perma.cc/AQ2N-WUCM).

4   McKinsey (2024) Analyzing the CEO–CMO relationship and its effect on growth, www.mckinsey.com/capabilities/growth-marketing-and-sales/our-insights/analyzing-the-ceo-cmo-relationship-and-its-effect-on-growth (archived at https://perma.cc/9K2E-V2J3)

5   McKinsey (2023) What is the C-suite? www.mckinsey.com/featured-insights/mckinsey-explainers/what-is-the-c-suite (archived at https://perma.cc/JPV3-Y39W)

6   Ibid.

7   Demandgenreport.com (2024). Demand Gen Report – your source for the latest B2B marketing news & trends, www.demandgenreport.com/ (archived at https://perma.cc/PAG4-CP8B)

1

B2B Content Marketing Strategy Needs a Refresh

I once consulted with a large, multinational B2B corporation that sold a suite of products to multiple buyer types and had multiple marketing teams: Corporate Brand Marketing, marketing by product, marketing by solution.

My assignment was to improve the performance and efficiency of marketing for one solution (which comprised several products that served a particular customer cohort) by refining their content strategy and production process, cross-functional campaign operations, and establishing a new modus operandi that could be used by marketing teams for other solutions and products.

One of the initiatives they were launching was a webinar series intended to capture ICP (ideal customer profile) leads. The campaign was designed to leverage internal and external channels and resources to maximize impact and efficiency, including:

- utilizing internal influencers as hosts and distribution channels
- containing a plan to atomize video afterwards into various content channels and campaigns
- a cross-promotion strategy with relevant business units with overlapping audience

They spent tens of thousands of dollars on paid media, allocated several team resources including me (an outside consultant), marketing strategists, developers (to create the landing page), mid-funnel team to craft post-webinar nurture, etc.

They mapped out a detailed customer journey that plotted touch-points and stages with messaging, channels, and outcomes, and a cross-departmental action plan with deliverables, dependencies, and deadlines. They even crafted a detailed plan for coordinating across business units and stakeholders, including weekly check-ins with everyone involved to ensure they launched the webinar—and all its promotional campaigns—on time.

The campaign itself had already been approved by the CMO, so all the marketing team needed to move forward was a sign-off from the Corporate Brand Marketing team that we'd adhered to corporate brand guidelines and a developer to build us the landing page (the core asset for the entire campaign). Not a problem—we'd accounted for that in our plan and had already prepared a summary for the corporate marketing and dev teams highlighting the campaign strategy, creative assets, copy, and a detailed developer spec to make the landing page.

(I know what you're thinking, and you're right: this is where it started to fall apart.)

First, our request for developer resources got knocked down the priority list at the last minute because the company needed them for another project they deemed higher priority. Fine, fair, it happens. However, when we did finally get our landing page, the most important part was missing: the call-to-action (CTA).

In fact, the developers *had* included it, only they put it at the very bottom of a page stuffed with "mandatory" content added by the corporate marketing team. To make matters worse we were only allowed one CTA on the entire page and, they said, according to the company's brand guidelines they were only allowed to put it at the bottom.

Visitors needed a search party to find the CTA.

The combined delay from the dev and corporate marketing teams meant we couldn't provide the landing page link in time to launch the paid media campaigns promoting the webinar.

The result of this was a detrimental impact on the campaign:

- without the link, we couldn't meet deadlines for our email ad campaigns, which meant we lost two valuable channels that our paid media agency had secured to assist webinar attendance goals;
- programmatic channel campaigns launched late, and we missed our attendee goal;
- organic, owned channel campaigns were also delayed;
- overall webinar attendance did not meet the target, so the post-webinar nurture campaign didn't have the same number of people, which led to fewer down-funnel conversions.

Despite the team initially deploying all the elements of a functional marketing plan that

- utilized internal influencers and the community;
- included partnering with other business units to increase campaign distribution;
- had a content repurposing plan to extend the impact of the campaign from both organic and paid components;
- templatized their approach to help them hit future targets by increasing the number of campaigns they could execute in each quarter.

Their campaign failed because of stodgy processes and overly prescriptive—and outdated—brand guideline practices, which led the company to lose money both in ROI of marketing spend and future potential revenue by:

- overspending on agency and consultant fees;
- compromising ad spend performance thus driving up customer acquisition costs (CAC) well above target;
- using more internal resources across departments than the project logically required, which not only destroyed the campaign's ROI but also delayed progress on the other projects those resources were working on.

Missing Targets

The company's leadership held the marketing team solely responsible for missing their quarter's KPIs and did not acknowledge any operational issues. As a result, they reduced the following quarter's marketing budget, leaving the team with fewer resources to hit a higher target and a defunct campaign plan that they had to completely recreate in order to execute on webinar campaigns that were already scheduled for the following quarter (which included highly paid internal influencers who had already begun production).

The End...

...of the most common B2B marketing story ever told.

How's "Doing Content Marketing" Going for You These Days?

Here's the reality: Content marketing represents one small part of company growth.

In fact, most of the content marketing "strategies" you've been creating are just project plans. This includes most of the keyword-driven content plans and the thought leadership content you create for your executives. The reason: You're executing the same tactics in largely the same ways as everyone else, so there's nothing inherently strategic about it. You may choose a different topic or hire a designer to make your content "prettier" or distribute it in a more unique way, but in most cases, you're not *really* doing anything different from anyone else.

FIGURE 1.1 Growth Strategy Marketing

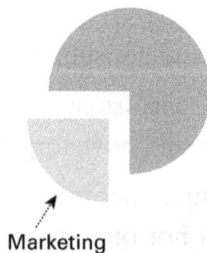

Marketing

And because we're all doing the same thing over and over expecting a different result, we obsess over things that don't matter, like the Oxford comma or AI-generated content, or what makes a piece "compelling." And gosh do we love our personas, journeys, and brand guides.

None of that matters as much as you think it does. Under my leadership, Animalz grew from a $1.8 million ARR business to over $12 million ARR in four years and we didn't even deploy the organic growth content strategy we used for our customers. We honestly didn't do much marketing at all. Yet we became one of the most in-demand content marketing agencies in B2B SaaS.

As a fractional CMO consultant, I've significantly grown annual revenue and margin for agencies and SaaS companies alike in a single quarter on little to no budget and without doing much, if any, marketing or reducing headcount (I often net increase it along with pay).

I know what you're thinking: this isn't marketing. That's the point!

What I'm trying to say is that there are more ways for content marketers to grow companies. We are not confined by the existing personas, journeys, channels, and tools. Our customers certainly don't limit themselves in that way. They are exploring, experiencing, and thus changing all the time. So why would we as content marketers remain static in our approach to reaching and connecting with them?

I'm going to spend the following chapters sharing different ways of thinking about growing companies and examples of growth tactics other brilliant marketers are experimenting with. I will also present frameworks I've developed from 15+ years serving hundreds of B2B companies, including some of the largest brands in SaaS, as a content marketing manager, director VP, and consultant, as well as the CEO of a content marketing agency.

But first, we really do need to check in on how content marketing is doing, starting with my favorite topic:

The Customer Journey

Most marketers are focused on where they want potential customers to "go."

So they create a map of how to get you there. And that map shows a straight path from a starting point to an endpoint with destinations in between (with squiggly lines going in and out showing types of content for some reason).

You've seen this model before—the marketing funnel, buyer's journey, or customer lifecycle. The details vary, but the approach remains consistent: Companies create a model of how they believe buyers should move toward purchase, then design marketing activities to guide them along this predetermined path.

If they can get you from one end to the other and you take that final action, then they win the game.

And to verify which destination you're at and where to take you next, they created these checkpoints and called them touchpoints (Figure 1.2). As you go along their journey, marketers track where you are on the path and how you got there so they know where to make you go next.

Basically, this linear touching map is supposed to help the company know how well you (their customer) know them, like them, and whether they've touched you enough times in enough ways to move you to the next step.

And marketers, we make all this happen! We create touching campaigns that are supposed to motivate as many people as possible to speed down this runway until the end when they finally "convert" into a customer. This is the creepy customer journey we have been following for a long time.

Only when I look at how humans make purchase decisions in real life, not only is the path not linear, I don't see a path at all! What I see looks more like Figure 1.3.

What if the journey is more like a subway map with multiple paths that connect and customers are traveling through those paths all the time? The map contains all possible paths and customers go on their own mini journeys through them. One day it's LinkedIn ad to webinar that I sign up for but don't attend. But I get the notification with

FIGURE 1.2 Traditional Customer Journey

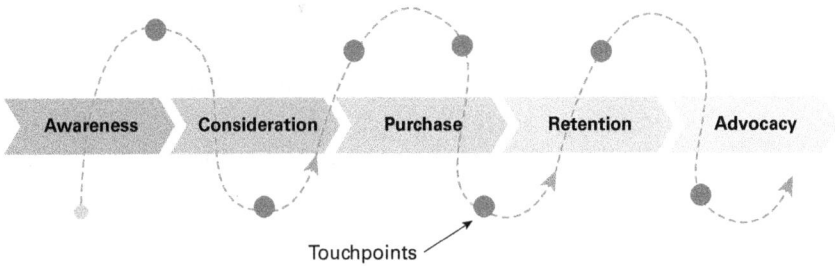

FIGURE 1.3 Chaotic Customer Journey

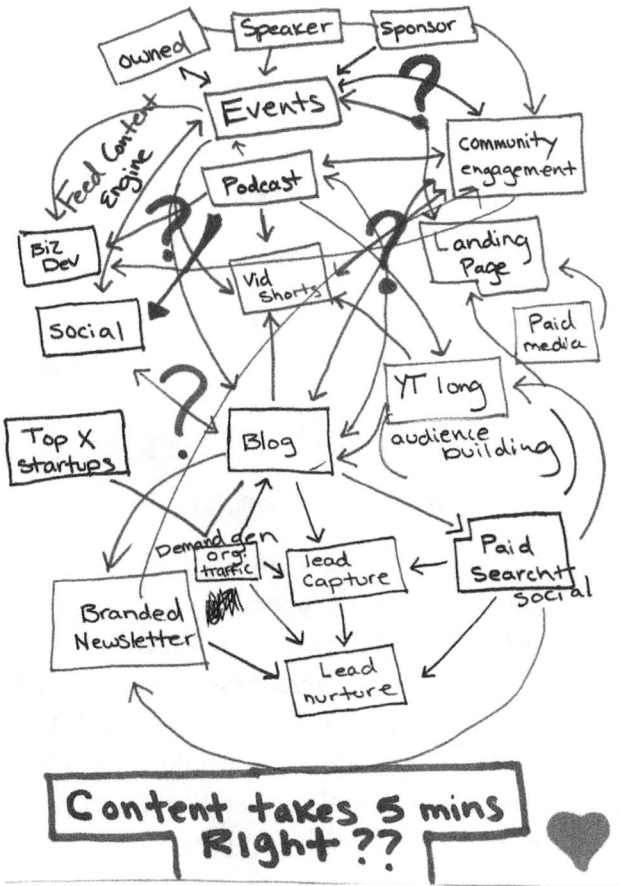

replay after, so a few days later I play it while scanning the transcript for the specific part I'm interested in. I like what I see so I click back to the homepage where I saw your newsletter and sign up.

Some paths turn me into a customer. Others make me a follower because I like your content, but another product works better for my company. I still advocate for you, I just didn't become a customer first.

While the subway map feels closer to reality, it's still too preordained, too preplanned. Life isn't like that and to expect work decisions to follow that path—or any path—doesn't make logical sense.

KEY POINT

"Very few qualified buyers will Google a category of software they need, explore the search results one by one, find a site they like with messaging that resonates for them, sign up for a demo, and buy the product without considering other options. That's just not how people buy, and it never was."

John-Henry Scherck, CEO, Growth Plays

Which made me wonder: What if customers aren't on a journey at all?

The Limits of Traditional Marketing Thinking

It's like we've all agreed to this standard concept of growth based on existing marketing tactics, tools, playbooks, and frameworks that we use to achieve a fixed—and narrow—set of outcomes.

And so we talk about how things have changed and how those changes affect our marketing strategy, and we're like, "Oh no, Google changed its algorithm again, what will we do?" or "It's the end of organic search traffic. It's the end of times!" because we're thinking about growth from the standpoint of an existing set of marketing tools, tactics, playbooks, platforms, and frameworks that we use in a limited number of ways to achieve a few specific outcomes.

This mindset creates three critical problems:

1 **We separate marketing from business growth.** Instead of seeing marketing as an integrated part of the business growth strategy, we treat it as a separate function with its own metrics and activities. This creates a disconnect between marketing efforts and actual business objectives.

2 **We limit our options.** When we confine our imagination to growing businesses through "marketing" as traditionally defined, we miss countless other growth opportunities that might be more effective, more efficient, or better suited to our specific circumstances.

3 **We optimize for activity, not outcomes.** We become so focused on executing marketing tactics—publishing content, driving engagement, generating leads—that we forget these are means to an end, not ends in themselves.

For business owners and leaders who don't have marketing backgrounds, this mindset can be particularly damaging. It leads them to believe they must implement a standard set of marketing tactics regardless of whether those tactics align with their business model, resources, or growth objectives.

Our Playbooks Aren't Working That Well Either

Marketing playbooks, whether intentionally or not, end up accomplishing two things for marketers and companies:

- teach marketers and business leaders how to do content marketing;
- reduce the cost of executing long-term by providing a detailed map to your destination.

Both seem useful, but the latter is a little more problematic than it seems. When you prescribe "a way" you remove the need for independent reasoning and create an environment where experimentation is inherently—and artificially—limited to a narrow set of options. And the subtle implication of this is that growth costs less when you *don't* innovate.

Going back to HubSpot and their inbound marketing playbook, it worked well for a lot of companies and marketers for a period. I myself used the playbooks and educational content from HubSpot, MailChimp, and other early SaaS "darlings" when I was learning how to be a content marketer while on the job.

But what happened is *their* growth strategy became content marketing canon.

HubSpot built a community by being helpful in a consistent, methodical way to digital marketers at a time when both the companies they worked for and the tools and platforms they used were in near-constant flux. They gave us A Way That Works.

Basically, a *component* of their bigger growth strategy was to own the B2B market, which they did *in part* by making themselves the perceived mother of content marketing. And they achieved *that* by creating marketing guides espousing relative short-term ROI tactics to VC-backed companies which, by nature of their funding type, puts them in a forced, perpetual growth spurt in their infancy that requires them to make constant progress on a shoestring budget and bad advice.

Why this matters: Because this book is about B2B Content Marketing Strategy and I'm telling you that the things in those playbooks aren't necessarily your only solution; in fact, they may not be the right solution for you at all. Playbooks are simply ideas other people and companies created as part of their growth strategy. It's content marketing. I know what you're thinking: *what's the problem, then?*

When you look at companies like HubSpot evangelizing their playbook, showing how it drove growth for them, they're leaving out something important: Their playbook was only one small part of their overall growth strategy.

They executed a long-term, multifaceted, well-funded growth strategy that included their content marketing playbook. But that playbook was supported by several additional strategic components:

- community building
- positioning and messaging
- expertise and connections among the founding team
- timing: they capitalized on change (i.e. search engines, online behavior, startup industry maturation and growth) to create unique growth opportunity

- strong founding team and early hiring choices
- good execution

The problem is, once something is out there that works, it can be hard to justify—or even be motivated to—coming up with something from scratch. (It's also, sadly, illogical in many cases. Especially when you learned how to do your job by following that playbook.)

Then there's a whole vocabulary for it, people make their careers on it, etc.—you know how the world works.

All of this is fine, *except*, a playbook isn't a strategy. It's an instruction manual for executing something. There may be principles within, but inherently, and specifically with the B2B content marketing playbook, it's just a list of activities strung together in a way that was optimized for the state of the internet when it was created.

This isn't semantics or even a campaign to cancel playbooks. I think they are incredibly useful in certain situations and have followed one or two in my career when I didn't know what to do.

What I'm saying is,

Playbooks aren't useful when you're responsible for strategy.

They may help you achieve incremental growth—at least for a while—but that's just a well-executed plan.

A strategy involves discovering where the water is already flowing downriver and finding the most efficient way of making it go faster. And by the time you're in a strategic role, ideally you have the basic skills and enough experience executing them—hopefully at a few different companies—that you are comfortable manipulating them in new and different ways that suit your objectives.

In other words: You kinda have to make it up.

Take, for example, "best" time to send an email campaign. There are lots of industry standards showing days of the week and times of day that are best. But if everyone else is following that logic, how strategic is it for you to follow? And anyway, wouldn't a more helpful question be, *I wonder what send time catches our customers at a time when they're already checking email and would logically be motivated and have the ability to actually open it, read it, take the action we want them to take?* Basically, whatever outcome you're trying to accomplish by sending the email in the first place.

Testing to figure it out and using industry standards as part of your test definitely helps. But blindly following big data sets doesn't always result in the most optimal results.

It makes sense why we (yes me too!) have followed these best practices. A lot of companies—especially VC-backed startups—aren't institutionally supported to experiment in general, but especially with marketing. "Test" to them equals time, specifically more time to see results and that makes them uncomfortable. It's also incorrect, because a marketing test often still yields results, it just may not match the results you're aiming for at first. The test isn't to find people to open your email, it's to discover the *optimal* time to send it so the greatest number of people possible open it.

That's part of the reason the simple question of "should you do this or that" typically boils down to a debate of opinions and industry standards rather than a customer data-backed hypothesis augmented by your own knowledge and experience, and let's face it, a bit of guessing.

For example, if someone came to me asking "Should I put an emoji in the subject line of my email?" My answer: I don't know. And I have questions:

- What is your hypothesis based on? Did you factor in things like your own knowledge of your community and the nuances therein?

- Have you looked at current email deliverability standards to make sure the deliverability gods won't ding your email as spam?

- Crucially, are there colloquial applications of the emoji that have a different meaning that your community interpret in that same way (and did you even check)?

- Most importantly: Do you believe that adding an emoji in the subject line will result in a significant enough increase in open rate that it's worth experimenting with or debating in the first place?

The boring truth is, most people know what they want—consciously or not—and when they recognize it, they are inherently motivated to click it, read it, engage with it.

The Way We Measure Success Isn't Working

The reality is that an effective marketing strategy includes activities in both visible and invisible spaces and delivers measurable and immeasurable ROI.

Understanding this reality, marketers smartly build strategies that cultivate both measurable short-term gains and harder-to-measure long-term advantages in part by accessing their ideal customers in the spaces where they already hang out. In other words, they help the flow of water run downriver.

The challenge in the B2B industry specifically, though certainly not exclusive to it, is that most leaders don't get it. They may say words indicating their comprehension but given how peeved leaders get about the what, how, and who of it all, they obviously do (I explore this in more detail in Chapter 12).

Consider word-of-mouth recommendations. Traditional analytics can't track a conversation between CTOs at a conference or a private Slack message between industry peers.

Not every activity in your marketing campaign needs to—or, I would argue, should—prompt immediate and measurable action. That's just not how people work. And marketing is all about human people, so it's confounding to me why anyone would expect it to be different.

That said, marketers do need some evidence to determine whether they should continue investing in the things they're doing. They're a signal, big or small, prompting you to keep going and indulge in more curiosity in that area:

- Is your brand and/or content referenced in industry discussions?
- Do prospects reference a campaign, video, series, or activation either regularly or in proximity to when it was launched?
- Are you seeing a trend in folks replying to your company newsletter more often in response to something you did?
- Are you noticing that the types of folks following your show and the comments they post reflect your intended audience and depth of engagement?

Not that your boss will be moved by any of this, but since this book is being printed by a publisher, you can at least point to An Official Text by a Person with Credibility who they will likely think is a man at first, which is also likely to work in your favor, sadly, but also, if it works... it's worth me saying all this out loud, including my crescendo:

> Metrics should inform strategy, not drive it. They're indicators of progress, not definitions of success.

By embracing this principle, you can experiment with new tactics and uncover perhaps more effective ways to grow (with a little trial and error, of course). It might mean:

- creating content specifically designed to spark private conversations;
- building relationships with community leaders who drive word of mouth;
- investing in long-term trust building despite measurement challenges;
- focusing on value creation over metric optimization.

Understanding this principle liberates us from the prison of predictable growth confined by its incremental progress and tracking customers' every move. It nudges us toward investing in activities that build lasting advantage, even when their immediate impact resists quantification—or perhaps can't be quantified directly at all.

In an age obsessed with data, this willingness to embrace the unmeasurable might be our most powerful strategic advantage.

Our Brand Guidelines Aren't Really Working, Either

Companies use things like brand guidelines to ensure customers have a consistent experience with them as they grow and expand their footprint across markets, channels, campaigns—any point at which a customer interacts with them. It's a means of scaling something that exists.

Think about it this way: At some point a person created a solution to a problem they were having. This solution caught on over time and some brand probably owned and popularized it, thus bringing it into the zeitgeist. Now it feels like having brand guidelines is The Way for companies to create a consistent brand experience at scale. It's taught as part of marketing and business school curricula and used in some form at most companies.

But is a static document with prescribed fonts, colors, logo mark design direction, writing tone, voice, grammar style, and all the other minute details they include, really the only solution to brand consistency?

Furthermore, are those the elements that your customer interprets as brand consistency or are they moved more by people at your company, an event you hold every year, a thing you created that changed the way they think?

And what about rebrands? I've been involved in several resource-dense, costly, time-consuming rebrands at companies where the primary outcome was the rebrand itself. Were they losing customers over their logo? Is it necessary to rethink the company's entire look and feel just because they're applying a different design concept in the app?

Rebrands are primarily useful for creating attention around change: a new strategic direction or product, stale companies trying to reignite or simply capture market share they've lost to newer companies entering their space, or changing brand perception if the company has gotten a bad reputation or they have unclear messaging and want to change the minds of a market that has interpreted their value prop due to the company's own lack of clarity.

But rebrands are strategic moves that should serve a company objective—both short- and long-term given the size and cost of the project—and considered against other, potentially simpler tactics that you've evaluated and determined could have comparable or higher ROI.

My point is that brand guides and playbooks are boiled-down solutions intended to *help* a category of companies or industries execute a process at scale. And even though they may work, they rarely produce results beyond what you expect. And what I'm here to say is that if you change your thinking to understand strategy, planning, executing, in a slightly different way, you can achieve more with the same (and eventually less) effort. This isn't some telemarketing claim that all your problems will be solved—they won't (sorry)!

Instead, what I'm offering is a *different* way to approach marketing strategy and the challenges that come with creating, socializing, and executing it that, at least for me, has consistently produced better outcomes. Not just in the project itself, but for me personally in my career in terms of elevating myself such that I went from Content Marketing Manager to CEO in less than 10 years (and skipped a few titles in between), as well as the companies I work for, and the folks I work with.

A New Approach to B2B Growth

When we focus on "doing content marketing" instead of growing businesses, our chances of creating an effective strategy are immediately hampered by:

Fewer options: Envisioning growth solely through the lens of marketing we blind ourselves to the full array of options available to us and limit our chances of success. This is especially damaging for B2B companies, where product experience, customer service, pricing structures, and partnership strategies often drive growth more effectively than traditional marketing activities.

Misplaced focus: Marketing playbooks consist primarily of actions—volume of content, frequency of posting, number of campaigns—with the assumption that these activities inevitably lead to results. This activity-oriented mindset creates the illusion of progress while often failing to deliver meaningful outcomes. Marketing teams celebrate launching campaigns, publishing content, and generating leads without rigorously examining whether these activities actually move the business forward.

Wrong success metrics: Optimizing for marketing metrics, rather than business outcomes like engagement rates and even lead volume, keeps us on a growth hamster wheel. Scaling growth by working harder using existing frameworks isn't strategic.

The solution involves a shift in how we approach growth using content marketing tools and the other resources and opportunities around us:

- start with business objectives, not marketing activities
- leverage unique advantages rather than following generic playbooks
- look for more impact from fewer actions
- create self-perpetuating momentum instead of requiring constant effort

When your goal isn't "doing marketing" to grow the business but simply, well, *to grow the business*, you will notice more options you didn't see before and unique approaches that create sustainable advantage. And the "how" is based on frameworks and principles that I've applied to create consistently effective B2B marketing strategies across different company sizes and types.

Each chapter will guide you through a key part of this approach. Here's how we'll get there:

Chapter 2: Principles of Good Content Marketing Strategy

Unlike static playbooks that leave little room for strategic, creative thinking, I'm going to share some principles that will help you think for yourself. Using these principles not only helps you figure out what to do, they are a built-in framework for making the case to stakeholders and getting them on board. In this chapter, I'm going to show you how to:

- identify and leverage unique advantages that competitors can't easily copy;
- create systems that produce exponential rather than linear results;
- balance measurable performance with long-term brand building, so you can build a path *out* of the rat race;
- confidently present a defensible strategy that executives will support.

Chapter 3: The Human-Centered, Multimedia Approach to Content Marketing

Traditional B2B marketing playbooks are blueprints for assembly lines that produce generic, white label content that takes up space in our digital landfill.

> *Nobody wants this.*

Thank goodness! To draw people closer, all you need to do is inspire folks to show up as they naturally are, and be motivated to connect with other human people who are also presenting as their organic selves, sharing knowledge, experiences, jokes, and memes in whatever spaces are most comfortable. This takes less work than trying to boss people around with your conversion funnels. This chapter will present:

- non-cringy ideas for sparking community around your product and brand that consistently outperform traditional marketing tactics and do not include you asking your developers to share some social post in a subreddit;
- how to leverage thought leaders in your company, including executives who are too busy or resistant;
- the role of multimedia content in building authentic connections and how to create content that aligns with how people really make decisions

Chapter 4: The Community Growth Framework

I've built communities among customers and teams at every company I've worked for. To me, it's a facet of content marketing strategy—one that gives you a lasting competitive edge, even in saturated markets and constantly evolving technology. This chapter explores how to build self-perpetuating growth engines through:

- creating active communities by elevating others;
- creating space where folks of all communication types can flourish;

- inspiring people to organically become brand advocates (and how to nurture them).

Chapter 5: Getting to Really Know Your Customers

Cookie-cutter audience research results in generic content marketing. You're not conducting a research study, you're getting to know human people. Forget competitive analysis and personas. We're going to learn how to talk to people and listen to them on a deeper level to inspire better ideas for how to serve them. This chapter includes:

- expert customer research frameworks that help you connect with humans, instead of studying them like mice;
- translating customer insights into strategic advantage;
- working with emotion to inspire customers to engage with your brand and product.

Chapter 6: Turning Knowledge into Resonance

With deep customer understanding as your foundation, you can craft messages that genuinely resonate. This chapter shows how to:

- develop a distinctive point of view that cuts through the noise;
- craft messages that speak to both rational and emotional needs;
- align your communications with existing customer beliefs;
- test and refine your messaging for maximum impact.

Chapter 7: Aligning Channel, Message, and Messenger

You're a matchmaker, now! Have fun with it. I'll help. This part isn't all transactional. There's creativity involved, experimentation and play. And while the list below looks boring, I promise I've included ways to make it more adventurous and fun:

- identifying the best channels to use;
- matching messengers to messages and channels;

- building integrated systems that reinforce key messages;
- measuring success across nonlinear customer journeys.

Chapter 8: Designing an Efficient Content Marketing Plan Using Media and AI

With strategy, audience, messaging, and channels aligned, it's time to get to work. But you're underfunded and have big ideas. Well, at least that was my situation at every place I worked! The truth is, you *can* make stuff more efficiently without becoming the Laverne and Shirley of content. In this chapter I'll share a few methods of doing more with less that won't make you want to quit your job:

- create once, deploy across multiple channels;
- leverage media and AI to produce better outcomes;
- build content systems that improve over time.

Chapter 9: Measuring and Reporting on Content Marketing Strategy

Don't underestimate the power that reporting can bring to honing your strategy, inspiring new ideas, and aligning stakeholders and your teammates around your vision. Reporting is more of an analytical and storytelling pursuit than it is about sharing data. After all, like everything else in this world, data can be manipulated to tell different stories if you know how to zoom in and out and upside down.

You know what it doesn't require? Expert math skills. *Trust me.* So I'm going to cover the things that will really help you, like:

- ways to show ROI for "unmeasurable" marketing activities;
- telling compelling and convincing stories with your reporting to various stakeholders;
- using reporting to enhance your ideas and strategy along the way.

Chapter 10: What Makes "Good" Content?

I'll give you the answer right now: Good content can be executed; it delights your customers in such a way that it motivates them to engage with your brand and product and recommend you to their peers.

This is one of those questions for which, to answer it accurately, I must hurl the dastardly "it depends" answer in a response that makes everyone itchy. Since this is my first book and I really do want you to like it, I do my best to fill in dependent moments with examples. You still won't go home with An Answer (that wouldn't be strategic) but perhaps you'll be inspired to come up with one of your own.

(At least, that's my hope.)

And while I'm at it, I'll cover these things, too:

- creating content that changes behavior and thinking;
- common pitfalls that make content ineffective;
- balancing creativity with strategic objectives.

Chapter 11: Securing Buy-in for Your Content Marketing Strategy

Implementing any strategy requires stakeholder support and, let's face it, organizational patience and courage. In this chapter, I offer you:

- techniques for turning internal skeptics into advocates;
- exercises for developing and strengthening creative ideas;
- methods for building momentum through small, strategic wins.

Chapter 12: Building a Content Culture: Cross-Functional Collaboration

This isn't a warm, fuzzy chapter about everyone getting along. Your strategy needs support from across the organization for it to work—an annoying yet absolutely true fact that all marketers have to account for as part of their job. In this chapter, I present tips for:

- creating productive cross-departmental collaboration;
- developing strategic partnerships with sales, support, product, and executives;
- overcoming common organizational barriers.

Chapter 13: What Happens When It Doesn't Go to Plan?

Even the best strategies encounter challenges and roadblocks. This chapter presents:

- how to approach common obstacles;
- methods for turning roadblocks into strategic advantages;
- stories that won't make you feel *better*, but hopefully a little less targeted.

Stick with me. Because when you stop trying to "do marketing," it directs your energy to the most impactful things you can do to achieve your growth goals such that, in my made-up world, the water is flowing downriver on its own and you're in a unicorn raft sipping chardonnay and eating chocolate chip cookies (at least that's what I would do).

2

Principles of Good Content Marketing Strategy

I'm nine years old, standing on top of a pile of cow manure at the Natick Community Farm, holding a shovel and giving directions to the boys in my group.

My parents had signed me up for the summer program (ahem, against my wishes) and this was our first task: Shovel a giant pile of cow poop from one location to another. As my two teammates stood paralyzed, I climbed to the top of the pile and took charge.

"You, start shoveling over there. You shovel over here," I ordered. "I'm starting up here," I said while standing knee-deep in manure.

The boys didn't skip a beat. They appreciated that I took charge when they felt lost, and more importantly, that I was willing to get just as dirty as they were. Nothing was beneath me (except the poop). I was giving directions *and* doing the work to help us finish the project *together*.

And while it looked like I was taking charge because I had it all figured out, the truth was, I didn't know what I was doing.

I hadn't, at that point in my life, shoveled a large pile of poop before, so I wasn't speaking with any authority. What I did was take stock of what was in front of me, decide on a path forward, then make it happen. I (apparently) didn't worry about the "right" or "wrong" way. I also (again, apparently) didn't fret about what my teammates would think about me taking charge. Instead, it would seem, I decided on a solution and made it happen. And that time my solution worked.

It wasn't until almost 30 years later when I became CEO of a content marketing agency that I understood the principle behind what I had done.

Things didn't start out so great. I took over as CEO of the agency I'd been working for the previous two years in March 2020. Despite asking for this job specifically and suggesting to the founder that I assume my new role months earlier than planned to help manage the pandemic—imposter syndrome struck me *hard*.

Interestingly, it wasn't the chaos of the pandemic itself that rocked me. For some reason, I felt confident that I could lead the team through a time of crisis. Here's a letter I sent to the company just six weeks into my new role:

> I've been CEO of Animalz for six weeks and under my watch, we've lost more MRR than any six-week period in the company's history.
>
> Not the brightest spot on a resume, that's for sure! Yet when my friends and family ask me how I'm doing, I tell them honestly: pretty good. This has not been easy, and I'm definitely worried about a lot, not the least of which is protecting the organization and folks within it who are now in my care.
>
> The thing is, there is a lot that is outside our control right now. I can't control what comes my way, but I can control how I respond to it. My choice from the beginning has been to respond with focus, flexibility, and a whole lot of compassion—particularly for myself.
>
> The core tenets of content marketing are helpfulness and authenticity, and in a time of crisis that is exactly what folks need. Add to that the increased desire for human connection online due to mandatory physical separation and the abundance of time folks have to consume content right now... the case for content marketing is strong.
>
> So, here's the question at the top of my mind as I think about the future:
>
> *In three years, what will we look back on and say, "That was the best most transformative thing we could have done for the business"?*
>
> I don't have the answer yet, and we may not know which of the things we try this week, next month, or later this year will be The Thing. But I'm looking forward to getting scrappy, experimenting, and seeing what sticks.

My hang-up, the thing that kept me up at night my whole first year as CEO, was something I could not see.

The way.

As a homeschooled kid with a GED, not SAT scores, a bachelor's degree in arts from a relatively unknown state school, no money or connections (my parents didn't either, but they loved me a lot and that made all the difference!), I'd spent my whole life feeling like there was a preordained path to life and I wasn't on it. If you followed the path throughout your life, it would lead you to all the right knowledge, milestones, and places you needed to succeed.

Since I hadn't done any of those things, I assumed I was lucky and that all other CEOs got their jobs because they followed that path and therefore had some treasure chest of knowledge, experience, and skills that made them fit to be CEO.

(It goes without saying that I have a thriving imagination, even as an adult.)

Clearly, I thought, I needed to consult a real CEO to figure out what I should be doing.

I spoke with a few CEOs I knew and while they all gave me helpful advice, when it came to the specific problem I was trying to solve at that time, they all had the same disappointing response.

After presenting them with the challenge I faced and the solution I proposed to it, they all replied with some variation of, "Yeah, sounds right."

"Sounds right?" I pushed back. *"Don't you know?"*

One CEO laughed. "No one knows. You just make it up and see what happens."

What's worse, several of them even asked *me* for advice! I was floored. "So, there isn't one single established way to be CEO?"

"Nope," they confirmed, seemingly unburdened by the same reality I found horrifying.

Once this truth sank in, everything changed. If no one truly knows exactly what they're doing, and there's no single "correct" way to run a business then I was the perfect person to lead the company, because I had no idea what I was doing!

It turned out I really was the perfect person for the job in large part *because* of my unconventional background. Turns out, the parts of me I'd always felt self-conscious about were the ideal preparation for a role without playbooks:

- being homeschooled starting at age five;
- attending a semester of college in Hawaii when I was 16;
- running a business at 17;
- getting into an elite college without a high school degree or taking the SATs (then going to a city school instead);
- interrupting my career for a year and a half to volunteer in Bali right when the B2B SaaS industry was entering its heyday.

You know what else my background prepared me for? Becoming CEO in March of 2020. It was my choice, actually. The founder gave me an "out." Instead of taking him up on it, I told him to move the transition timeline up: "The team is going to need someone to get them through this, and you're not it." (No shade, he knew what I meant: We each had our own strengths. He supported behind the scenes, and the entire leadership team worked together to keep the company afloat without laying anyone off.)

The first six weeks were wild. We hemorrhaged customers to the tune of over $100,000 in monthly recurring revenue. Then the trend flipped on its head and because we'd built so much credibility in the years prior, we were one of the most in-demand content agencies in B2B SaaS. We had a three-month waitlist and our biggest challenge was finding and keeping talent, learning how to scale a company from 18 to 130 people and annual recurring revenue from $3 million to almost $12 million.

I'm not bragging, I'm making a point: It doesn't matter what your background is and you don't need to be prepared to succeed at most things (I'm just saying, being a CEO is pretty easy compared to going to space, which I'm pretty sure you need LOTS of preparation for).

What you need is curiosity, bravery, tact, and a whole lot of patience if your "thing" is marketing, because for some reason in B2B specifically, marketing is incomprehensible to most of the people in charge. The principles I outline in this chapter are tools you can use along the way. You'll still have to deal with the same challenges, and some of what I suggest will probably make people mad, but what I'm offering you is more useful than getting a budget approved or alignment on a strategy.

I'm offering a different approach and way of thinking which, once you get the hang of it and adapt it to your personal style, you can use to change your circumstances more often than you are currently (anyone promising more than that is selling snake oil).

It turned out, while I was still "making things up," the years of doing just that were the best experience for leading through the unknown.

Why Content Marketing Programs Fail

Besides the outside forces challenging marketers, there *are* some they create for themselves. And I only know because I was one of them, so consider this me trying to help you avoid some of the mistakes I made. Common mistakes marketers make that lead to disappointing outcomes include:

They Mistake Motion for Progress

- Emphasizing "how much work they did" instead of the outcomes of those actions which only makes them look less strategic.
- Avoiding learning how to analyze quantitative and qualitative data, causing them to miss out on improvements to their strategy and new ideas.
- Not connecting their work to broader business strategy due in part to inadequate understanding of measurement (and development of their analytical skills).
- Executing "best practices" or pursuing trends without reasoning from the circumstances.
- Misplaced perfectionism: focusing on arbitrary quality standards (can we all please relax about the Oxford comma?) rather than efficacy.

Meanwhile, business leaders fall into traps of their own.

They Confuse Novelty with Wisdom

- They don't support their marketing teams. Without leadership buy-in, even the best marketing strategy struggles to gain traction. Or they consider the marketing department an in-house agency that responds to internal demands and a growth org that is assigned its own KPIs.
- They waste their marketing teams' resources and budget on impromptu tactics they learned from a friend or a newsletter without considering whether they will have the same ROI for their business.
- They have unrealistic expectations. Many promising marketing strategies are abandoned before they can logically show results. Or the strategy is showing positive results but it doesn't look the way they thought it would, so they think it's bad.

Both groups miss a fundamental truth: Tools, behaviors, and tactics evolve, but strategic principles are constant. They change only when you decide to change them. That's what makes principles so valuable—they stand the test of time.

> *Without leadership buy-in, even the best marketing strategy struggles to gain traction.*

As a business grows, the macro environment changes as well as the company itself. That is why leaders and marketers need adaptive strategies that capitalize on timely opportunities, enable constant experimentation, and maintain progress toward growth goals.

Favoring Growth Activities over Outcomes

Too many business leaders are asking the wrong questions about growth.

They fixate on tactical questions: Should we start a podcast? Do we need to be on LinkedIn? How many blog posts should we publish each week?

These questions seem logical to them, because tactics are concrete and actionable. They promise quick wins and clear metrics. But leading with tactics creates a weak foundation that crumbles under pressure.

I've seen this pattern repeatedly during my career, especially when speaking to CEOs/founders and marketing teams at small companies all the way up to large enterprises. When I asked them, "What outcome are you trying to achieve?" they often gave tactical answers:

"We need to double our organic traffic in Q3. Our board wants to see rapid growth in pipeline metrics."

"What's your opinion on gating or not gating an ebook?"

"Our competitor is dominating the top three search positions for 'sales automation software.' We need a content strategy to outrank them in the next six months."

"I need to drive more MQLs this quarter since our paid channels are becoming too expensive. How quickly can we launch an SEO-driven content strategy?"

"My content team is only publishing two long-form pieces per month. Our competitors are putting out content daily. How do we scale production to match their velocity?"

The problem with these questions: They are tactical, not strategic. A strategic question would have centered on business outcomes:

Founder: *We need to increase revenue by X% in H2 and show we have a sustainable marketing engine that can scale to Y revenue so I can secure my next funding round.*

VP of Marketing: The CTO has been put in charge of marketing and believes marketing is pointless. I was just given millions in budget and approval to hire 15 people. Now that the team is ready, I need to show exponential impact in the next month or my budget and headcount will be cut next quarter. What are the highest-impact activities that will show results in the first three weeks while building toward long-term success?

Chasing content marketing tactics—whether it's long-form SEO content, influencer partnerships, or generative AI—is likely to bring initial success, but it won't last without strategic principles to help you maintain momentum as the company grows.

Adopting a Strategic Mindset

I learned a lot about being a better marketer from running a company. I finally understood some behind-the-scenes stuff that drove leadership decisions that didn't seem logical to me before. (Don't get me wrong, most of the decisions you think are stupid still are. I'm just saying, the smartest person in the room isn't the one talking; they're listening with a warm face while gathering the information they need to get their way.)

But that took a backseat to the real benefit. It turns out, though, that the same mindset that I developed from running a successful business also helps create better marketing strategy. It consisted of the following (in no particular order):

Be curious. Start with a blank slate:

- Recognize that industry best practices are just someone else's made-up solution that became popular.
- Question conventional wisdom with curiosity and don't judge. You'll still annoy a lot of people, but they won't think you're a jerk, which is important because you'll need their help when you're trying to get buy-in.
- Focus on principles, not prescriptive actions.
- Measure what matters, not just what's easy to track.

Be brave. Experiment. Fall on your face:

- Create an approach that others can't easily copy.
- Get over your fear of being wrong—and the potential consequences of it. The best way to do that is to advocate for your ideas until one of them is approved and try owning whatever happens instead of

placing blame elsewhere. You might be accurate, but you won't learn anything from it.

- Own your decisions even when it makes you feel uncomfortable. You'll gain more respect and trust by being curious about what went wrong than pointing fingers.

B2B Content Marketing Has Changed

Modern content strategy is no longer about being a brand megaphone, shouting messages across digital space.

Modern content strategy that works is a blended approach designed to create community around shared experiences, build lasting relationships, and establish genuine trust and influence. It's about leaning into individuality within niche communities by creating content that resonates with individuals and small groups rather than trying to appeal to the masses.

And it's definitely *not* a pursuit of ubiquity, in the ways brands used to do it by creating a dominant presence on every platform and community space.

Instead, it's about taking fewer actions to accomplish more, playing a supporting role in the community sometimes by elevating others. It's about building relationships that motivate action rather than force it. Mostly, it's about creating frameworks and principles to guide and evaluate your decisions so you can develop your own "playbook" that works for your company and community.

Principles of Good Content Marketing Strategy

Content marketing exists to serve business goals by solving customer pain points. It accomplishes this through education and relationship-building:

Education attracts potential buyers and influencers by providing immediate value in the form of short-term solutions (awareness and affinity).

Establishing trust allows your brand to become an ongoing part of your community's lives by speaking their language, empathizing with their challenges, and solving their problems (nurture and engage).

Relationship formation creates alignment between external promises and internal experiences—the product delivers on the expectations set by content (convert, grow LTV, and upsell).

The goal is to help first and sell second—at which point customers often feel they reached decisions independently. They become eager to invest in both the product and the relationship. This is how content marketing works organically based on human behavior.

It's also the stuff you already know.

Content marketing teams guided by the following principles consistently achieve superior results.

Create Unique Advantage

No other company exists with your exact combination of product, people, and resources. Your first job as a marketer is to identify what you already have that can be leveraged for growth.

This could be your founder's network, your CMO's substantial LinkedIn following that overlaps with your target buyers, or a product feature that solves a previously unaddressed problem. It might be an upcoming conference where your CEO is speaking to 300 decision-makers who gather only once per year.

Other advantages might include:

- budget, software, and technological resources
- existing audiences, email lists, or content archives
- market position (whether as an established leader or disruptive newcomer)
- opportunistic events like funding announcements or key hires
- your own unique talents, experiences, and connections

The goal is to create a content strategy that:

1 competitors can't easily duplicate because they lack your specific advantages;

2 generates exponential impact by leveraging opportunistic events, efficient execution, and activities that serve multiple outcomes simultaneously;

3 is scalable with repeatable elements that compound over time and can expand with relative ease.

A prime example comes from Gong, the revenue intelligence platform. While competitors focused on standard SaaS marketing playbooks, Gong leveraged their unique advantage: access to millions of sales conversations and the data patterns within them. By sharing insights from this proprietary data, they created content no competitor could replicate, establishing themselves as the definitive source of sales intelligence while simultaneously demonstrating their product's value.

Serve Outcomes It Can Logically Impact (Better Than Other Approaches)

Strategy that serves business goals does need to be measured to ensure it's serving those outcomes, and ideally how well it achieves them. Yes, I'm talking about ROI.

The benefit of having clearly defined, quantifiable, time-based outcomes is twofold:

- it helps you narrow down tactics
- it gives you a target to "bump up against" to extract learnings for continuous improvement

---

REAL-WORLD EXAMPLE
Outcomes over Deliverables

When I was CEO of Animalz, I instilled the philosophy of "outcomes over articles" into our client management operations. It was the principle that, no matter what customers asked us for or we delivered, we had to frame it in terms of the outcomes (goals) they were trying to achieve. Seems obvious, but people's memories are short, so instilling it as a principle helped me create a mindset on the team that would influence how they operated organically.

And we applied it starting with our very first interactions with clients: the sales call. When a customer said to me, "I want thought leadership content," my response was, "Why?" What I was really asking was, "What outcomes are you trying to achieve with thought leadership?"

I recall one client—an Insurtech company—hired us to increase lead form completions. Their customers were insurance providers, the majority of whom still managed much of their paperwork and processes in an analog fashion. They also weren't digital first in their product discovery. Instead, they traded recommendations at industry conferences they all attended annually. At these events, companies still distributed printed materials to potential buyers.

Armed with this knowledge we left out common tactics like search content and social distribution and proposed a strategy involving printed assets coupled with personalized digital follow-up. So instead of approaching their problem from the perspective of the services we provided, we focused on the outcomes they wanted, in this case, an exact number of form completions by quarter-end from their ICP.

This principle forces you to evaluate each potential marketing activity against a simple standard: Is this the best way to reach the business outcome we want, or are we doing it because it's the way we've always done it?

Can Be Executed with Existing Resources

A strategy is only as good as your ability to execute it.

Your plan is only strategic if you factor in all constraints, including budget and resources. If you come up with a "brilliant" idea that you know is unlikely to be funded, then it's not brilliant in the context in which you want to apply it.

So, if you come up with something that could really move the needle and you want to get funding for it, come up with an MVP and call it a test. Once you've shown impact and dazzled the purse-holders, then it'll be easier to get budget to expand and do more. So start by getting buy-in on only those resources you need to execute a bare minimum version that demonstrates enough impact to justify additional investment.

One approach that has worked for me (though it's not a silver bullet) is to treat it like a sales activity. All I need is enough of the right kind of information that whomever I'm pitching to will:

• understand without a complex explanation

- see a type of business impact they recognize as valuable
- not care too much about it (i.e. the investment is negligible to them)

Your best-case scenario at this stage is not enthusiasm; it's disinterest. You want them to feel like saying yes is an errand, almost like it's a waste of their time.

This requires keeping a ton of details to yourself—especially the ones your leadership will question. Also useful, make it feel familiar and demonstrate you listened to them by pointing out areas where you intentionally factored in something they wanted or advised. Think of it like landing page copy. Your "conversion" is a yes, so what message and supporting details will convince them to click the yes button?

This doesn't mean your strategy can't be ambitious. Rather, it means being realistic about what you can sustain long enough to see results.

Serves Outcomes It Can Logically Impact (Better Than Other Activities)

It doesn't matter what size your marketing team is—at some point, you'll be tasked with showing impact beyond what seems possible with your current resources. This is where strategic thinking becomes essential.

Content marketing strategy plays a crucial role in driving business results. What sets a strategy apart from a simple plan is its ability to serve as a unified and thoughtful response to a significant challenge, as emphasized by Richard Rumelt in his book *Good Strategy, Bad Strategy*.

A plan is simply a list of activities you know you can accomplish, like running errands in a particular order to minimize time. Strategy, by contrast, is leveraging your resources to produce a desired outcome beyond expectations in some way (such as time, cost, results). Then you use your success as leverage to secure the budget and buy-in you wanted in the first place.

This doesn't mean your strategy can't be ambitious. Rather, it means being realistic about what you can sustain long enough to see results that you can use to do *more* later.

Grounded in Facts, Not Best Practices

Choose channels, tactics, and messages based on YOUR customers, not on what others are doing or what industry best practices dictate.

At some point, nothing we currently do in marketing existed before. SEO, for example, was once considered a growth hack. It wasn't in the content marketing lexicon, let alone on any list of best practices. Someone discovered it could provide a unique advantage for their company to appear first when people searched for specific solutions.

This principle requires you to reason from your specific facts:

- How do YOUR customers make purchase decisions?
- What channels do THEY genuinely use for discovery and research?
- What unique circumstances does YOUR company face?

What might appear as constraints—limited budget, market position, team size—can often become advantages if you approach them with curiosity and objectivity.

Designed to Have Exponential Impact

Most "strategies" content marketers present are just action plans that itemize tactics they will execute over a period of time to hit a goal.

> *Create content, distribute it, convert people, measure results, repeat.*

But think about how content marketing itself came to exist. It was all about leverage. Take SEO, for example. It was essentially a "free" way to get more people to visit your site without paying for ads. And for a while, it was an ROI multiplier, meaning that the amount of investment required to execute was miniscule compared to the long-term impact it would have over time. That's a strategic ratio.

Now, SEO is a part of B2B marketing modus operandi. The ratio is more incremental, thus it's not really a strategic activity, it's more of a table stakes tactic.

The opportunity for marketers *now* is to come up with a scalable way to transform bespoke interactions between people from the company and community across multiple mediums into ROI for the company that they can sustain. This means designing your strategy such that some activities serve more than one purpose or outcome, as well as having "self-sustaining" elements (i.e. automations, work-flows, etc.) built in.

START WITH MEDIA (VIDEO OR AUDIO)

Rather than starting with keywords and blog posts, build your production plan around a single video and break that into multiple assets—and asset types—to suit your community and the platforms where you're sharing them.

Remember content clusters? What if you took the same approach to production? Only instead of starting with an article, you start with a video (or several) capturing interviews from folks on your team and in your community that you can later break up into the assets you need. A single video interview might become a podcast episode, multiple blog posts, social media snippets, and an email newsletter—each strategically utilized to achieve your target outcome(s).

For example, say you determine that leveraging your CEO as part of your strategy will be instrumental in achieving the outcomes you're responsible for. You know the CEO is busy and it's hard to write content on their behalf. Record an hour-long video or even several shorter videos over multiple conversations then break that into quotes, captions, clips, and tips to share in a community Slack.

The most important thing when starting with media: If part of your plan is to use it on a media platform like YouTube, make sure you know and capture the elements that cater to how folks consume on that channel. Have your checklist of phrases or intros you need them to recite and make it feel like a quick errand.

STRATEGIC CHANNEL SELECTION

You don't need to "be everywhere."

Focus your energy on the spaces (channels) where your audience is already hanging out; build relationships and earn credibility by contributing net new value (not the thinly disguised brand bait your leadership team is pushing) then you can build on that foundation to expand into brand-owned spaces. If you've done a good job, in my experience, the community ends up asking *you* to do more, which changes your task from pushing a rock up a hill to opening a dam and letting the water flow downriver.

COMMUNITY-POWERED GROWTH

The most powerful exponential effect comes from community engagement. When your content strategy centers on real people—both internal subject matter experts and external community members— you create natural ambassadors who amplify your message through their own networks.

The key is to design your strategy so that today's content investments become tomorrow's growth drivers. Your community should help create content that attracts more community members, who in turn create more content. Your media assets should spawn multiple pieces of content that drive traffic back to your core message. This compound effect is what separates sustainable content marketing from exhausting content creation treadmills.

Embraces Experimentation

Experiments help you identify new working approaches that haven't been proven but might produce outsized results. This requires:

- comfort with uncertainty
- willingness to fail publicly
- ability to learn quickly from results

I recommend a portfolio-style spread in your marketing activities where the bulk of your resources are directed at activities to cover your objectives but leave some room to try new things. The following breakdown is not a science, but gives you an idea of what I'm talking about:

- 70% proven tactics that reliably deliver results
- 20% evolved versions of proven tactics
- 10% experiments

Experimentation isn't random—it's guided by your strategic principles and tied to specific outcomes. Each experiment should test a clear hypothesis about how a particular approach might drive better results than established tactics.

The experimental mindset separates truly strategic marketers from those who simply execute playbooks. It creates space for discovering your company's unique path to success rather than following trails already blazed by competitors.

Applying These Principles to Create Your Strategy

When these principles work together, they create a strategic foundation that will guide your decision-making and provide built-in, business-focused justification that your leaders will understand. It will also reduce the impulse to chase tactics or pile on activities. Instead, this framework will help you achieve your business goals and customer needs efficiently:

1 Establishing outcomes aligns your strategy with both customers and the business.

2 Unique advantages can accelerate results and/or increase impact.

3 Grounding in facts validates your approach.

4 Starting with existing resources proves your approach works (so you can ask for more investment).

5 Designing for exponential impact maximizes your efforts.

6 Connecting qualitative results with outcomes demonstrates there's business in more than just what's easy to track.

7 Embracing experimentation continuously improves results.

Use these principles as decision-making filters when building, evaluating, and getting buy-in for your content marketing strategy to make your path to executing a little smoother.

And for those pesky "opportunities" or tactics that come your way from across the company, use a truncated version with the person suggesting them. Bringing them into the evaluation process helps them see for themselves whether their idea is worth pursuing *right now* or not.

IMPORTANT NOTE ON EXECUTION: For this to work, you *must* check your attitude at the door. Put your facilitator, problem-solver hat on when posing these questions. You *must* make it clear with your face and your voice that you're trying to reason it out *with* leadership, not argue. They are going to become agitated and annoyed by these questions, because most likely they haven't thought their idea through and don't know how marketing works (despite believing they do). To make this go well for you, keep an even tone regardless of how emotional others become. I recommend deflationary tactics like:

> "You seem upset. Can you help me understand what I'm doing to upset you? My goal is to help by reasoning through the idea with you."

> "My intent with these questions is to explore your idea by checking the boxes I need to determine if it's viable and when to prioritize it. Understanding the business case, cost, ROI etc., enables me to suggest potential solutions to any roadblocks before we reallocate resources to execute it."

> "What if we tried your idea on a smaller scale as an experiment? Here's what that might look like."

The most important thing is that you be as genuine as you've ever been in your life in this conversation. Leaders can tell when you're being fake. The folks who come across as the most disingenuous are the ones who have spent the least amount of time being curious about corporate norms and instead judge how things are without truly knowing what they are judging. And I'm telling you, for your benefit, *we can tell*, even if we don't show it. That's just us doing a better job of being more professional than you.

And I'm saying this not to judge *you*, but to help *you* (yes you, too) manage a common and tricky situation for *your* benefit. This advice is from personal experience. I've been a total brat at work in ways that only got me fired. I'm trying to help you be yourself *and* get your way which, in the work context, does require some expressive compromise.

- Will this impact our P1 business objectives this quarter? If so, will it accomplish our objectives better than the strategy we're already implementing (factoring in the time and money costs of changing course at this time)?

- What facts and/or assumptions is this idea based on? If their answer doesn't include current companywide assumptions or facts about your ICP, then ask them to tie it back to them.

- Why should we choose this over our existing strategy? Which aspects of our current strategy do you recommend we stop doing so we can execute on your idea?

- Can you show me what you project the ROI will be from the initiative and in what way it serves our P1 objectives for the quarter?

- Do we have the resources on hand to execute this strategy to the depth required for it to be successful? [If not] will you provide the resources we need to execute?

- Will it show impact in the time we have left in the quarter to hit our P1 objectives?

This filtering process prevents common strategic mistakes. For example, many B2B companies launch podcasts because "everyone has a podcast." But without running this decision through your principles, you might miss that:

- your audience prefers reading to listening
- you lack the resources for consistent production
- the format won't create exponential impact

Instead, applying these principles might reveal that your strategic advantage comes from your engineering team's deep technical expertise. This could lead you to focus on detailed technical content that can be atomized across channels, requires fewer resources than a podcast, and builds genuine trust with your technical buyers.

The principles also help you avoid the trap of tactical thinking masquerading as strategy. As my mom always says when I need help getting unstuck, "Just because you have an idea doesn't mean it's important."

True strategy isn't just a collection of best practices or a list of channels to pursue. It's a coherent approach that:

- maximizes your specific strengths
- addresses real customer needs
- creates sustainable advantage
- scales efficiently with resources
- generates compound returns

Most importantly, these principles free you from the endless cycle of chasing marketing trends. Instead of wondering "Should we be on the latest social platform?" or "Do we need more video content?" you'll evaluate opportunities through the lens of first principles, which set you up for success much better.

Common Mistakes to Avoid When Applying These Principles

Even with solid principles in hand, it's easy to make implementation mistakes that undermine their effectiveness.

Mistaking Common Capabilities for Unique Advantages

"We have great writers" or "Our CEO is well-connected" aren't unique advantages—they're table stakes in B2B SaaS. A true unique advantage is something competitors can't easily replicate.

For example, a fintech company with early access to transaction data from emerging markets—that's a unique advantage. Their well-designed website? Not so much.

Equating Volume with Impact

The most effective strategies concentrate resources on a few key objectives that, when achieved, naturally unlock a series of wins. But those objectives must be realistic given your current capabilities and resources.

Trying to do everything at once dilutes impact. The companies that grew fastest were those that identified their critical leverage points and focused intensely on those areas, letting the ripple effects amplify their success.

Abandoning Strategy Too Early

Good strategy requires patience. The principles in this chapter work—but they rarely work overnight. Many companies abandon promising approaches just before they would have started showing significant results.

Commit to your strategy long enough to properly evaluate it (typically 6–12 months minimum), while maintaining the flexibility to adapt based on what you learn.

Failing to Adapt

Principles remain constant, but their application must evolve with changing market conditions, technology, and customer behaviors. Regularly revisit how you're applying these principles, even as the principles themselves stay consistent.

Conclusion: From Principles to Practice

Throughout this chapter, we've explored the foundational principles that differentiate good content marketing strategy from bad. These principles aren't revolutionary—they're grounded in timeless strategic thinking—but applying them consistently will set you apart in a landscape dominated by tactical execution.

Remember:

- create and leverage unique advantages
- focus on outcomes your activities can logically impact
- balance measurable and immeasurable elements
- design for maintenance with existing resources

- ground your approach in facts, not best practices
- build for exponential rather than linear impact
- embrace constant experimentation

In the following chapters, we'll move from principles to practice. We'll explore how to implement these ideas through human-centered content creation, efficient media production, and community building.

But first, let's address a question you might be asking: "If these principles are so effective, why don't more companies follow them?"

The answer is simple: It's harder. Following established playbooks is easier than developing your own strategic approach. It's safer to copy what others are doing than to chart your own course. It's more comfortable to focus on what's measurable than to embrace the ambiguity of what's valuable.

Strategic thinking requires courage—the courage to question assumptions, to try approaches others aren't using, and to persist when results aren't immediate. It demands the curiosity to look beyond best practices to your specific circumstances and customer needs.

In other words, it requires you to recognize that everything in marketing is made up—and then to make up something better.

3

The Human-Centered, Multimedia Approach to Content Marketing

I'll never forget the time a customer called me ugly.

To be fair, he said my profile picture in Gmail was ugly, but still, how rude!

I was working in customer support for a startup and productivity app called Springpad. He was mad because a bug in our free software app prevented him from doing something he wanted to do.

Back then I used to brag about how I could make anyone love us, even the people who were most angry, so I was happy for the challenge. In my reply, I started and ended with a bit of humanity.

"Hi, I'm Devin, a human person who has been helping you with this problem. What you said hurt my feelings. The bug you're dealing with, I understand why it's frustrating! I'd feel the same way if it was blocking me, too. I'm on your side, trying to help you. So please, no more insults, ok?"

He apologized, revealing that his mom had just died, and he didn't mean to take it out on me. And, not that I needed it, he added that I looked pretty in my profile pic.

By then I wasn't surprised by his response. I was accustomed to the way some customers acted when shrouded by their computer screen, which is why I developed responses like this intended to humanize both of us and get them collaborating with me.

After a while, working with users 1:1 and in support forums, I cultivated a group of enthusiastic "power users" who loved our app and would beta test new features, give us feedback, and help other folks in the community when they had questions about the product.

These newly minted fans even created their own Google Plus group about Springpad that I and other employees at Springpad participated in. Users shared tips, hacks, bug reports, and feature ideas, as well as asking us questions.

One of the group's creators was a Springpad champion named Art Gelwicks. He was already deeply embedded in the productivity space and loved our product. Aligning his personal brand with Springpad gave him a unique angle that differentiated him from other influencers in the productivity community. So, when he came to me and pitched cohosting a YouTube show about Springpad-based productivity I was all in.

"You and I recognized from the very beginning the power a community has on the recognition and adoption of a tool," Art recalled as we reminisced about the show. "So many companies do not recognize the power of their advocates and their willingness to be partners in growing adoption of their product."

That alignment in principles between community creators is crucial to both attracting people and motivating them to engage. And there's one principle that has been the leading driver of success for all the communities I've built, whether for a company or my industry. Your purpose must be veritably altruistic. That means getting buy-in from your boss as well as campaigning to senior leadership that what you build is crucial to ROI. It does take time.

When I approached Springpad's CEO, Jacqueline Hampton (the first person to give me a job in marketing!) with Art's idea, I was upfront about early business impact (none) while also making the case for why that was a worthy short-term investment.

This is a dramatic retelling of what I said, updated with improved language and argument structure, so it's more useful to you. In truth, I think what I actually said was, "I want to do this thing," and Jacqueline asked follow-up questions that I answered clumsily and almost certainly without tying it back to revenue:

> The show won't impact revenue—or my own goals— for about three months, and I don't yet know exactly what role it will play in either at this moment. My hypothesis is that it will be a source of user acquisition and retention in the future, but for now it's an experiment to see if it's worth pursuing.

Given that, I've mitigated risk through project constraints. We will launch one show per month, leverage the community and existing marketing assets (like our newsletter) to promote it, and use existing equipment (a hodge podge of lamps, piles of books, and furniture). I will also maintain my assigned work, so the experiment doesn't compromise the goals I've already committed to.

KEY POINT

Offering additional personal time isn't a necessary concession to getting buy-in. In my case, I was a junior content marketer who was career motivated and felt strongly enough about the idea—and the benefits to me if it worked—that I felt fine offering. This isn't always the best course of action and perhaps more a sign of my lack of executive management skills than anything. But it does work in a pinch.

From the beginning, Art and I maintained a casual, approachable vibe. We recorded live on Google Hangouts (aka YouTube) and didn't edit them afterwards. Art shared productivity hacks and asked questions the community wanted answers to; I gave honest answers to his questions, often including behind-the-scenes context to help explain features we hadn't prioritized or bugs we weren't going to fix.

"I remember a time on the show when I brought up a feature Springpad didn't have, and you offered a workaround," Art recalled. "I responded saying something like, 'Yeah, that just doesn't work,' and instead of making excuses or continuing to push a workaround you knew didn't really work, you responded, 'Right, that makes sense. We (Springpad) need to rethink this.'"

These simple, nerdy face-to-face conversations humanized both the company and the community. Art was an unofficial ambassador for the community, as was I in the context of this show. The sincerity of the environment and the authenticity of both the show and us as hosts was one of the biggest reasons the show resonated with folks from the beginning.

"The important thing was that it wasn't a company show," Art emphasized. "A company show was not going to gain any footing, but creating something that felt like an equal representation from user and employee had a much better positioning."

One of the things that made Art such an effective messenger was his dual positioning. To the Springpad team, he represented our power users—the people who pushed our product to its limits and shared in-depth feedback. To the community, he was a trusted expert as well as a Springpad champion who shared the unique productivity solutions he discovered but also didn't shy away from noting the places where we fell short. This commitment to honesty on both sides extended to the community group as well, where Art made a point of maintaining high standards for constructive feedback.

"When looking at forums like Reddit, they can be bastions of negativity for most products," Art noted. "We wanted our Google Group to be a moderated environment where we facilitated solution-based conversation for the whole community where dialogs became brainstorms rather than a stream of complaints.

"I had a couple of conversations with people in the community who posted gripes like, 'This feature is terrible!' I would DM those folks and say, 'Look, I appreciate that you have strong feelings about this. However, that doesn't help anybody else in the group. What do you think would be a better option? Put that out there.'"

Springpad leadership, including its founders, understood the value of nurturing the community and had created a user-focused culture from the very beginning. This made it easier for all our community initiatives to succeed, in a few ways.

First, I didn't have to waste tons of time getting buy-in or making up numbers to represent the value of community building, which isn't designed to be measured 1:1, action to ROI, in the first place. Coming from a corporate background, Jacqueline thought both short- and long-term and believed in making strategic bets, even if we didn't have tons of evidence to back them up.

"You were always good at coming up with crazy ideas that cost us nothing but could create some buzz," Jacqueline remembered. Nice compliment, but more importantly, it represents a growth mindset that a great many startup founders never fully grasp.

Second, the founders and founding team had built customer-centricity and community building into company culture from the start. And instead of making empty pledges in our messaging and values, they simply acted that way from the start by incorporating the community in their operations, from engineering and product through customer support to marketing.

They understood the business value of community building and what "good" brand participation looked like. For example, I didn't need to convince my boss that joining the Google Group was more advantageous than trying to "own" it or use it as a direct sales channel. She knew that would just alienate the group's members and get us kicked out.

In fact, Springpad supported the community in multiple ways. It became part of my daily customer support checks, so questions didn't linger unanswered. Our head of product participated, asked the group for feedback, and resolved bugs folks reported. When we fixed something or were launching a major app update, we told them first.

For Springpad as a company, the show provided:

- direct user feedback in a public, constructive format
- increased product adoption through peer-led education
- a dedicated testing group for new features
- authentic advocacy from trusted voices in the productivity space

For community members, it offered:

- access to company insights without corporate filtering
- practical solutions to their day-to-day challenges
- connection with like-minded productivity enthusiasts
- a voice in the product's development

Even after I left Springpad, members of the Google Group still wished me happy birthday until they sunset the app. It also left me with several lessons for modern B2B content marketing:

- **Authenticity is sticky**
  We built trust that translated into loyal users and advocates by engaging in honest conversations about both our strengths and weaknesses.

- **The right messenger matters more than the perfect message**
  Art's position as both community member and company advocate
  gave him credibility that no amount of marketing polish could
  achieve for a company representative unaffiliated spokesperson.

- **Channel selection should facilitate conversations**
  The combination of YouTube and the Google Group created
  spaces for both synchronous and asynchronous connections that
  served different community needs.

- **Empowering the community creates self-reinforcing growth**
  As the community took more ownership of helping each other and
  directing conversations, the marketing effort required from the
  company actually decreased while impact increased.

This alignment isn't a one-time exercise. It's an ongoing process of
listening, experimenting, and adapting. But when you get it right—
when your messengers are authentic, your channels serve your
community's needs, and your message focuses on genuine value—you
create marketing that doesn't feel like marketing at all.

And that's when the real magic happens.

Community Growth = Company Growth

Community growth strategy is inherently aligned with company priorities.

Content marketers have seen this hamster wheel play out for years:
They are hired to make content on behalf of the brand and thought
leaders at the company, which they publish and then ask folks at the
company to promote it from their own social accounts, regardless if
they have followings related to your product.

Meanwhile, your coworkers are already engaging in online and
offline communities where your potential customers are hanging out,
building relationships based on shared industry and experiences. The
wealth of ideas, content, and relationships they are organically generating is still a largely untapped opportunity.

And, confoundingly, what many company execs still don't see is how a community growth strategy is inherently aligned with their priorities.

Efficient and Exponential

It is cost-effective for companies of all sizes to leverage existing resources, automation, and generative AI to produce more content. You don't need a huge budget. For marketers who are always fighting for buy-in, as well as resources, community-based growth allows you to try before you ask the company to buy.

Multiple voices cover more ground more efficiently, especially when paired with a media-first approach leveraging AI to atomize content into different formats, lengths, and styles. And once you've established yourself as a positive contributor in the community, growth begins to happen organically through word of mouth (WOM), invitations to speak at events, inbound partnership opportunities, and more.

Reduces Customer Acquisition Costs

According to a study by Bain & Company, acquiring a new customer can cost 5–25 times more than retaining an existing one.[1] Community-driven growth leverages existing relationships to reduce this cost dramatically.

Solves For Long Sales Cycles

In B2B particularly, where purchase decisions can take months or years, community engagement maintains connection and builds trust throughout the process.

Builds Lasting Trust and Influence

This trust advantage translates directly to business results and is more powerful than anything money can buy. When people hear about your solution from a trusted individual rather than an advertisement, they're significantly more likely to consider it seriously. Highlighting their insights as part of our marketing strategy was an opportunity to build a bond and trust with potential customers and aligns with how modern B2B decisions actually happen.

Is Adaptable

It's flexible enough for your employees and community members to talk about your product and brand in their own words, positively and negatively, while still retaining its fundamental form and definition.

(I know, I know, your brand team is screaming. PR already created a smear campaign to discredit me. CEOs everywhere just put a temporary ban on all marketing. And content marketers? Meanwhile, y'all are rolling your eyes like, "Duh, tell me something I don't know.")

Reduces Risk

When you incorporate your customers, buyer community, employees, leaders into your B2B content marketing strategy, you create an organically differentiated approach to the market that will make you stand out from your competitors. Brands will live "forever" in the conversations around your vision, values, product, and the people behind it.

Even if a competitor takes the same approach, they still won't be able to create an identical experience, because they won't have the same people. Think about it: If no two people are exactly the same, then doesn't that make them one of the only things in the world that can't be copied? Why not leverage them more in your marketing, then?

Especially look at what people naturally gravitate towards and are intrinsically motivated to participate in. They're consolidating their online communities into sub-sub-groups. They are curating their feeds. They are increasingly chatting with a small group of trusted friends in group texts or Slack groups. Or they are in a subreddit with

hundreds or thousands of anonymous people who are deeply passionate about a topic.

It's Hard to Copy

In a world where competitors can duplicate your features, copy your
messaging, and mimic your tactics, community becomes your most
defensible advantage.

There is no one way to "do community," which creates inherent
leverage for you. For example, say part of your strategy for building
community as an established brand is to consistently reply to small
follower accounts on Bluesky or another emerging platform. This
creates connections that can't be algorithmically replicated or copied
through a standard playbook.

While tools like video and AI are essential components of a modern
community growth strategy, they aren't what will separate you from
the pack, because they are available to all businesses, no matter their
budget.

Humans, while also a resource that every company can leverage in
their growth strategy, cannot be copied (at least not yet!). Their
unique perspectives, experiences, ideas, and personalities are organic
differentiators. This includes your customers, employees, and others
in your industry—even sometimes your competitors themselves.

When I was the Director of Content at Help Scout, we launched a
community-driven campaign designed to celebrate folks in the
customer support industry. We called it Humans of Support, a riff on
the popular Humans of New York photoblog created by Brandon
Stanton in 2010. We didn't shy away from featuring customer support
folks from competitor companies. The opposite, in fact: I saw it as a
sign of strength and commitment to our mission to include them. (It
was also a conversation starter with potential customers at conferences by recruiting contributions for the series there.)

This may seem obvious, but it bears repeating: Platforms are just
spaces for people to gather online. Platforms can prompt engagement
and help you find connection opportunities. But they can't inspire
you to connect. They can't even really motivate you to connect on
their own.

They need HUMANS and CONTENT (created by humans) to make you take action.

This reality is why frameworks that produce exponential content in an efficient way help B2B companies grow faster, even those with smaller budgets. By focusing on human connections rather than platform mechanics, you create content that resonates on a fundamental level.

How Human-Centered Content Differs from Brand Marketing

Traditional content marketing is distinctly brand-centric. It's characterized by:

- strict brand guidelines that prioritize consistency over authenticity
- a single brand voice used across all communications
- structured approval processes that slow down publication
- a heavy focus on polished, professional production
- corporate messaging developed by committee

Human-centered content flips this approach completely:

- flexible guidelines that allow for personal expression within brand parameters
- multiple voices, each with their own style and perspective
- streamlined approval processes focused on accuracy and value, not perfection
- authentic production that prioritizes substance over polish
- messaging that emerges organically from customer conversations

This isn't some sort of employee handbook that teaches everyone how to talk about the brand, or a forced social media calendar consisting of topics and tone that clearly aren't relevant for every person at the company to share. It's a framework that draws out each contributor's individuality and connects it to the community and your company.

Media Compounds Community ROI

The mistake many companies make is viewing community- and conversion-focused marketing as separate strategies. They strengthen each other tremendously.

"Conversion-focused marketing efforts (e.g. promotions, retargeting) are attractive because they're easy to quantify and can be helpful in gaining quick sales. But they do little to attract new customers, and they can lead to brand erosion when used outside of a holistic marketing strategy," according to Nielsen's 2024 Annual Marketing Report.[2]

Think of community as the foundation that makes all your other marketing more effective and media as an amplifier. When people already know, like, and trust your company through community interactions, they become significantly more receptive to your conversion-focused campaigns.

Video

Not only is YouTube the most used social platform among US adults (85 percent) according to a 2024 Pew study, it also sees dramatically more use compared to LinkedIn (35 percent), which is a go-to for a significant portion of B2B companies.[3] While the broad strokes of this study likely show a larger chasm between the two platforms than actually exists among B2B buyers, YouTube's platform data shows an increase in B2B buyers consuming work-related content, and marketers have for years been seeing impact on brand awareness and other KPIs from YouTube.

And that's just one video platform.

Additionally, these platforms continue to add both free and paid features that help individuals and brands build audiences on their platform and generate impact from their followers through selling product, getting sign-ups on owned properties, making subscription revenue from their video, as well as the traditional ad revenue.

There are also education and course-building media platforms that not only provide the infrastructure, templates, and hosting for video courses—many have created their own communities in which to embed your course for increased distribution.

And, of course, these are only the more public platforms. Companies like Wistia and Loom are tools that marketing, sales, and customer support teams have been using for years to have more personalized, async conversations and get better conversion rates on outreach.

PODCAST

Rachel Downey, *Founder and CEO, Share Your Genius*

A podcast is both a channel and a piece of content. As a channel, your podcast feed engages your audience directly. As content, every episode becomes a catalyst for creating videos, blogs, graphics, and more. This dual role makes a podcast uniquely powerful. For lean teams with limited resources, it's the engine of a media-first strategy that can ripple across your entire business.

Think of it like this: Your podcast is your radio station. The episodes are long-form content that lives on the feed and fuels everything else—short-form videos, LinkedIn posts, blog articles, and email content for your campaigns. When done intentionally, a podcast becomes your brand's central hub for creating content that meets your audience where they are and how they prefer it.

And here's something unique: A podcast is one of the few mediums your audience can engage with while commuting, exercising, or simply stepping away from their screens.

Audiences aren't actively seeking your brand's content; They're looking for connection. No one is begging for more content. "Better" doesn't mean people will actually consume what you create. Podcasts aren't just episodes. They're storytelling tools that create connection, a form of communication deeply ingrained in us as humans.

It's not about how many people listen to the episode; it's about how deeply the story connects with those who do. Each episode becomes an opportunity to build trust and start meaningful conversations, and those two things combined is what drives business outcomes.

But success, like anything else, starts with clarity. Before you press record, take the time to define:

- What's the business outcome we're solving for?
- Who is this podcast for?

> • How will we measure success?
>
> Without clear answers, your podcast can quickly become just another task on the to-do list—or worse, a mandate from a CXO chasing the latest trend (and who's too busy even to sustain it).

Why More Companies Don't Do Community Right

If human-centered, community-driven content is so effective, why isn't every company doing it? The answer is simple: They can't see what success looks like.

Product-led companies and founders often can't envision community success because it doesn't fit neatly into their product-centric worldview. VCs don't like risks, so they go with what they've seen work. CFOs insist you can't measure it, so it's impossible to track.

Other types of B2B companies are similarly held back due to operating in an antiquated industry with leaders who are used to traditional tactics, or constraints due to regulation, or they are, like their SaaS counterparts, not incentivized to take even small risks.

When I consult with marketing teams, I often hear the same objection: "Our leadership wants something more predictable." The irony is that human-centered approaches are often more predictable in their long-term impact, even if they're less structured in their implementation.

Yet because many B2B leaders still don't understand the fundamentals of modern marketing or community building, they are limited by simply not understanding—or believing—the metrics that demonstrate this type of strategy is working. This makes it difficult for B2B marketers to make the case for and report on word-of-mouth strategies.

REAL-WORLD EXAMPLE

Community in Action: Balloon Seltzer

My friend Juliana LOVES seltzer.

She loves it so much that she launched a craft seltzer company called Balloon.

As a career B2B Saas content marketer, Juliana took a community approach to building the brand and began campaigning while the seltzer itself was still in development. She used LinkedIn and email to tell her founding story as it was unfolding and capture early interest in the product.

When she had a prototype ready, she launched a pre-order campaign that she shared with her professional community, friends, and family to get early feedback on the formulas of her first three flavors before selling them to the general public.

Juliana's authenticity and openness drew a lot of people in and made them feel part of her journey. She even shared setbacks with us, including a time when she had to delay the first shipment of pre-orders because of an unforeseen complication. The community she'd built around the product and her founder journey rallied around her even more, turning a potentially tricky situation into one in which loyalty only increased.

As she continues growing her business, she participates in private online communities of e-commerce business owners, exchanging knowledge, resources, and support. She attends local events around Toronto, connecting face-to-face with potential customers and retail partners then sharing in her personal and professional online social spaces.

In the summer of 2024, she ran a "Fizz Fest" event in collaboration with a handful of other local beverage brands to draw attention to the sparkling water scene in Ontario, attracting new fans for Balloon by co-marketing with more established brands in the space.

When regulations around direct-to-consumer imports came into question, Juliana spotted an opportunity for newsjacking—getting herself featured in *Business Insider* by offering expert commentary on how policy changes would impact small brands like hers.

Each of these approaches cost little to nothing financially but yielded tremendous value through relationship-building. Unlike paid advertising that stops working the moment you stop paying, these community connections compound over time.

Another strength of her approach lies in its sustainability. By aligning how she funds her business with the way she wants to grow it, she can go at the pace she wants without external pressure from investors. This path isn't just more financially accessible—it's often more enjoyable: Juliana gets to celebrate wins with people who've been part of her journey from the beginning.

And the results speak for themselves: She launched a functional, growing direct-to-consumer business with loyal customers and complete ownership that is well-positioned for strong retail sales and profitability in 2025.

For B2B marketers, Juliana's story offers a powerful reminder: Community-driven growth isn't just an alternative approach—it's often a superior one for creating sustainable, values-aligned businesses that weather economic uncertainties. By prioritizing genuine connections over rapid expansion, founders like Juliana build businesses with stronger foundations and greater resilience.

Conclusion: From Human-Centered to Human-Powered

Throughout this chapter, we've explored how the human-centered, multimedia approach to content marketing creates authentic connections that directly impact the business's bottom line. This approach isn't revolutionary—it's based on timeless truths about human behavior and trust—but implementing it consistently will differentiate your brand in a landscape dominated by generic corporate messaging.

Keep in mind:

- leverage multiple voices from across your company and community
- create living audience profiles that evolve through constant interaction
- focus on genuine expertise rather than polished corporate content
- build systems that encourage word of mouth and organic sharing
- use multimedia formats to capture and distribute authentic insights
- design for both trust building and conversion

Remember, it's humans that set you apart from everyone else because no two are the same. Brands live "forever" through individuals in the community talking about your vision, values, product, and the people making it.

Notes

1 Cummings, A R (2023) Does it still cost 5X more to acquire customers than to retain them in 2023? Hashtagpaid.com, https://hashtagpaid.com/banknotes/does-it-still-cost-5x-more-to-acquire-customers-than-to-retain-them-in-2023 (archived at https://perma.cc/FJT6-QUFF)

2 Nielsen (2024) 2024 Annual Marketing Report, www.nielsen.com/insights/2024/
maximizing-roi-in-a-fragmented-world-nielsen-annual-marketing-report/
(archived at https://perma.cc/K7KC-5FB5)

3 Pew Research Center (2024) Social Media Fact Sheet, www.pewresearch.org/
internet/fact-sheet/social-media/ (archived at https://perma.cc/2WYT-RCUA)

4

The Community Growth Framework

Let's face it: your brand moat isn't going to be dug by your tech stack.

Agentic AI isn't going to hack audience growth for you and pixel data is no replacement for knowing someone's personality.

As ads and marketing content continue to bury us all in a digital pile and genuine opinion versus paid recommendation becomes increasingly difficult to parse, humans have—for a while—increasingly turned away from listicles and back to human beings when they want to know what to buy. Especially in B2B.

In the early days of content marketing, the concept of "produce high-quality content and deliver value to customers" was a novel growth strategy. It was supposed to be our post-swindle era of marketing ushered in by tech companies lauding principles like transparency and customer-centricity, when every department became [*something*] ops and every initiative was [*something*] driven. (I think of it as a commercial low point that being genuinely helpful to your customers was new and laudable, but at least some good came out of it!)

Today, if you aren't operating from this principle already, you face a commonsense issue, not a complex business challenge.

Technology alone won't save the day, either. With the volume of free and affordable tech available, there is virtually equal access among companies large and small to tools that enable efficiency. Meanwhile, marketers and SEOs are adapting to AI quickly and using it to create their own unique advantage and sharing their ideas within their communities, making AI another democratized solution rather than a competitive edge.

And the most widely used search engines quickly adapted their existing quality principles to incorporate new challenges presented by AI:

- Shift from "anti-AI" to "pro-quality": Most search engines are moving away from a stance that automatically penalizes AI-generated content. Instead, they are focusing on rewarding high-quality content that meets user needs, regardless of how it's created.

- Emphasis on human oversight: While AI can be a useful tool, search engines generally emphasize the importance of human oversight to ensure content is accurate, original, and provides value.

The bar is higher and it's been there a while, so if you're only using traditional content marketing tactics for your growth strategy, then you're way behind.

The Community Exponent

The thing about growth is that companies want it to happen in two somewhat conflicting ways: exponentially and predictably.

Guess what? Those two things don't stay together throughout the lifetime of a growing business. Predictable, scalable growth is where your playbooks are already assisting you. While you will continue to augment your predictable growth process over time to respond to market changes, technology changes, customer behavior changes, etc., your scalable systems are like your foundation. And even though they require constant maintenance, they are in the category of automated growth tactics, even though there's likely a great deal of manual process involved in running them.

The exponential growth—the "growth hacking", if you will (but, now that I mention it, please don't)—requires a different kind of engagement in order to spot the opportunities at the right time, and act on them in bespoke ways that draw the community to you in a positive way.

Rather than "hacking," which implies brief strategic interactions, community building is a constant hum, one that folks across the company can incorporate into their routine. No more marketing as an internal agency. Implementing a community growth strategy at your company looks more like clearing the way for water to flow downriver rather than the outbound hamster wheel of swimming against the current.

And the great news for executives is that it often requires less budget to facilitate the participation of their team within communities than it does to launch a campaign, and given that folks are interacting with their communities on a regular basis, there are more frequent and low-stakes opportunities to run experiments.

DON'T JUST FILL FEEDS. FULFILL NEEDS

Brooke Sellas, *Founder & CEO, B Squared Media*

Trust is built through engagement, authenticity, and responsiveness. Social selling isn't about cold DMs or aggressive sales tactics; it's about creating relationships through valuable content and genuine conversations.

FIGURE 4.1 Digital Customer Lifecycle

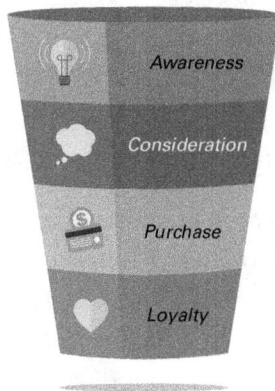

Traditional Customer Lifecycle

Awareness

Consideration

Purchase

Loyalty

Digital Customer Lifecycle

Watch Banner Ad

Shop Online

View Print Ad

Watch Tutorial

Watch Video on Mobile

Purchase via Call Center

Blog

Download App

Watch YouTube Ad

Compare Online

Purchase In-Store

Post Reviews

Read Reviews

Purchase via Mobile

Like on Facebook

SOURCE Brooke Sellas, B Squared Media

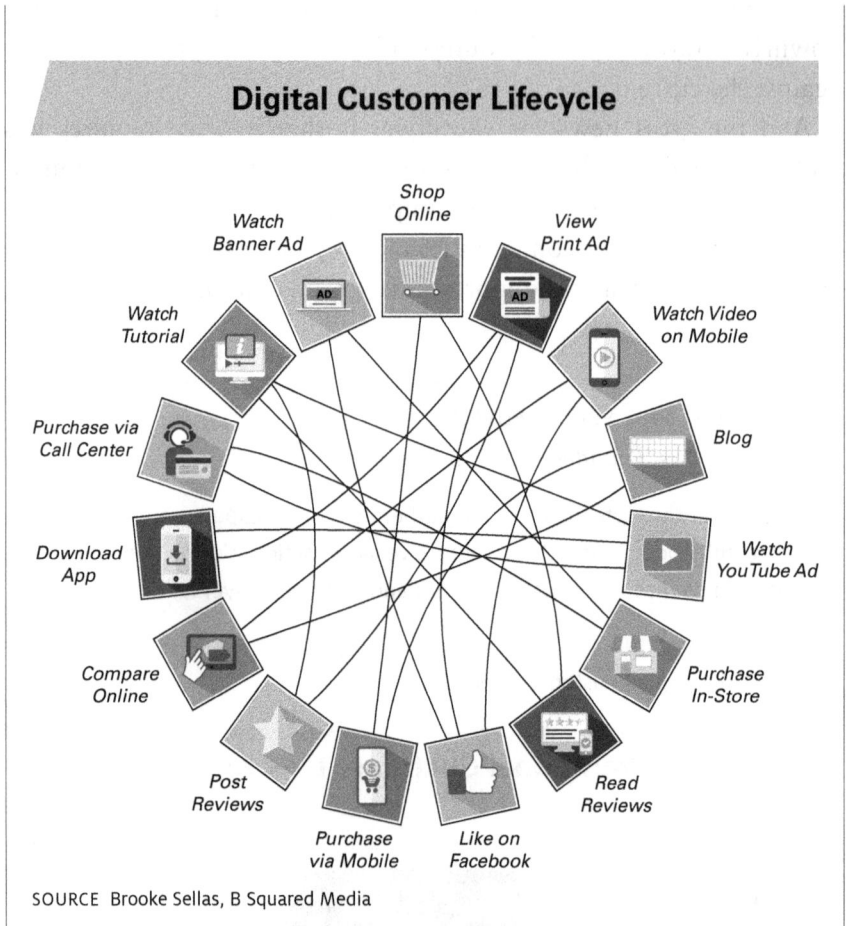

Community Is Your Strategic Advantage

How do I create a content marketing strategy that capitalizes on unique advantages (internal and external) to produce predictable growth and increase opportunities for exponential impact leveraging existing resources but can also easily scale and contains short-term measurable tactics that leadership will recognize as progress?

In Chapter 2, I talked about the principles that make up good content marketing strategy. The community growth framework inherently applies those principles as well as the tactics of the human-centered, multimedia approach and will lead your company to achieve longer-term, higher-value outcomes:

- Solves for long sales cycles and reduces customer acquisition costs by keeping potential buyers engaged and invested.
- Builds lasting trust and influence through human expertise that leaves a halo around the brand even when employees leave your company.
- Creates sustainable competitive advantage: It doesn't matter if your competitors are there too, because no one can copy the folks at your company who are participating.
- Doesn't rely on technology or trends: Platforms come and go, but folks stay together based on common interest.

Remember that moat you wanted to build? Once you've established yourself as a positive contributor in the community, you're no longer an external brand talking to potential customers. You're humanized by the folks who work there and represent the company in their communities, making it easier to bounce back after a blunder (actually, if the company is listening to the community it can avoid most blunders altogether).

Not only that but growth begins to happen organically through word of mouth (WOM), invitations to speak at events, inbound partnership opportunities, and more.

This happens because operational aspects of a functioning growth system (the tactics, tools, and processes outlined in most content marketing playbooks) facilitate ongoing, bespoke interactions between people at your company, your customers, and the community. These interactions come from building genuine connections between people who share common challenges, aspirations, and expertise.

This is the power of a community growth framework—a self-reinforcing system where community engagement drives business and community growth.

REAL-WORLD EXAMPLE

How Private Dinners Drive Enterprise Sales

When Capsule, an AI video editing tool for enterprise companies, needed to reach creative directors at major corporations, they faced a common B2B challenge: How do you build relationships with high-value prospects in a crowded digital landscape?

Their solution wasn't to double down on cold emails or LinkedIn ads. Instead, they went analog—organizing intimate dinners in cities across the United States. The results spoke for themselves: What started as an experiment became their most reliable sales channel, generating two to five qualified opportunities per event, with a 30 percent close rate.

THE STRATEGY: CONNECTION BEFORE CONVERSION

Natalie Taylor, Head of Growth at Capsule, describes their approach: "We knew we wanted to sell to enterprise. Capsule was built first and only for enterprise companies. We had a very specific type of person we wanted to reach, and we knew getting into a room with them would be the best way to build a relationship at this stage of our company."

The team identified in-house creative leaders as their ideal customer profile. These were the people feeling the pain point most acutely—creative teams inundated with video requests from across their organizations, from marketing to internal comms to sales enablement.

Their outreach was straightforward: "We message people cold with copy like, 'We're hosting a VIP dinner for senior creative leaders centered around video and AI. Capsule is an AI tool that helps teams edit brand-compliant videos.'"

THOUGHTFUL CURATION

What makes Capsule's dinner series work isn't just getting the right people in the room—it's what happens once they're there:

- **Assigned seating:** "After the first dinner, I started assigning seats and had people switch halfway through, which helped everyone connect with more attendees."

- **Balanced messaging:** "Initially, we didn't sell hard enough. We were just broadly asking, 'What does everyone think about AI and video?' Now we come in a little firmer on why we're hosting the dinner and where Capsule fits in this landscape."

- **No product demos:** "Some people who come to dinner expect us to do a full-blown demo, but it would ruin the vibe. We want it to have this balance of just having fun, connecting with peers, and talking about shared interests and challenges."

- **Real-time collaboration**: "During the dinner, we're Slacking each other—'I have solid next steps with these two people' or 'I've warmed this person up, can you try to get next steps with them?'"

These dinners create a setting where authentic conversation happens naturally. "It never feels aggressive," Natalie explains. "People come knowing a little about what we do and asking questions. We set it up in a way that's enticing for them personally, but with enough context for them to naturally engage with us about Capsule and problems related to what we solve."

ANALOG = ATTRIBUTION AND ROI

The dinners cost roughly $5,000 each (about $7,000 including travel expenses for team members)—a modest investment compared to the returns.

"This is the clearest marketing attribution I've ever dealt with," Natalie shares. "We're so targeted on who comes and so intentional about getting the right people there that this almost always leads to outsized sales returns."

At a dinner in San Francisco, they connected with the creative director at ServiceNow, who became one of their strongest champions. In Boston, the head of video at HubSpot solidified a relationship that had been building through a pilot. By tacking onto Adobe Max in Miami, they landed Paycom as a major customer.

Beyond direct sales, the dinners create ongoing ripples. "It has all these compounding effects," says Natalie. "I have several people I now email and ask for intros to others: 'Hey, we're doing a dinner in Portland, saw you were connected to these three people—would you pass along an invite?'"

After 12 successful dinners in 2024, Capsule is tripling their investment in this strategy.

WHY IT WORKED

The approach works because it addresses multiple marketing objectives simultaneously:

- **Awareness:** Introducing their solution to the right people in a memorable setting.

- **Relationship-building:** Creating authentic connections with decision-makers.

- **Sales acceleration:** Shortening the sales cycle through natural conversation.

"Just reaching out cold and asking for a demo was not going to be as effective," Natalie reflects. "This approach gives us a compelling ask—it's just dinner, around a topic everyone is excited and confused about, with an opportunity to network with peers."

In a digital-first marketing world, Capsule's success reminds us of a timeless truth: Sometimes the most effective channel isn't a new platform or technology—it's direct human connection in the right environment.

And when you focus on genuine value for a small group first, you build the foundation for organic growth that can scale far beyond your initial circle. Through genuine conversations, using insights to design interactions that solve real problems, you create meaningful connections that compound over time.

The Community Mindset: Slow Your Role

Here's what a lot of companies get wrong when trying to build community: They expect results too quickly and they try too hard to control the outcomes from the beginning. Community building is a long-term investment that compounds gradually, then suddenly. The key is maintaining consistency in your approach while the framework builds momentum. This requires a different mindset than the traditional marketing journey. When you reach the tipping point, the community starts growing at a much faster pace:

- **Environments** (~~channels~~): Moving from channel-centric thinking to creating environments where your audience naturally engages.
- **Meaning** (~~metrics~~): Balancing short-term performance metrics with long-term brand and relationship building.
- **Community** (~~content~~): Shifting from one-way content broadcasting to facilitated community connection.
- **Specificity** (~~scale~~): Focusing on reaching the right people deeply rather than everyone superficially.

Throughout this process, maintain focus on these critical factors:

- Be yourself: Your community must genuinely serve member needs, not just business goals. Be transparent about your role and motivations.

- Consistency: Communities need reliable touchpoints and clear expectations. Establish regular rhythms for engagement and stick to them.

- Autonomy: Give members agency in shaping the community. Create frameworks that enable independence while maintaining quality.

- Value creation: Every interaction should create value for participants. Design activities and programs with clear benefits for all involved.

Building Your Community Growth Foundation

Now that you understand the framework and why it works, let's talk about how to start building your community growth foundation. This isn't about implementing all four steps at once—it's about creating the conditions for success.

Start with Your Existing Advocates

Every company already has community assets—people who love what you do and want to see you succeed. These might be:

- power users who push your product to its limits
- long-term customers who've grown alongside you
- industry peers who share your values and vision
- team members with authentic industry connections

Start by identifying these natural advocates and understanding what motivates them. What makes them passionate about your solution? What challenges do they face that you help solve? What kind of recognition or support would they value?

The mistake many companies make is trying to build a community from scratch when they already have the seeds of one waiting to be nurtured.

Focus on Value Exchange, Not Extraction

Communities fail when companies view them primarily as extraction opportunities—ways to get more value from customers without giving enough in return.

Successful communities are built on mutually beneficial value exchange. For your community members, this value might include:

- access to exclusive expertise or insights
- connection with peers facing similar challenges
- recognition for their knowledge and contributions
- early input into product development
- professional development opportunities

For your company, the value includes:

- deeper customer relationships and loyalty
- authentic advocacy and word of mouth
- invaluable product feedback
- rich insights into emerging customer needs
- a talent pipeline of people who already understand your space

Remember, this isn't a zero-sum game—the more value your community members receive, the more they'll naturally reciprocate.

Start Small and Intentional

You don't need to launch a full-scale community program on day one. In fact, that approach often backfires because you haven't yet learned what your community truly values. Instead, start with small, intentional experiments:

- host a virtual roundtable with your most engaged customers
- create a private slack channel for beta testers

- invite power users to co-create content with your team
- feature customer expertise in your newsletter
- organize a dinner for local customers and prospects

These smaller initiatives let you test assumptions, build relationships, and develop the skills your team needs to facilitate community effectively. They also generate quick wins that can help secure leadership buy-in for larger community investments.

Remember Art and the Springpad Show? We didn't start with a fully formed community strategy. We began with a single experiment—a live show featuring a passionate user—and built from there as we saw the positive response.

REAL-WORLD EXAMPLE

Navigating the Future of Google and Reddit's Influence[1]
by Ross Simmonds, CEO, Foundation & Distribution.ai

In early 2024, Google updated and rebranded Search Generative Experiences (SGE) to AI Overviews (AIO) alongside their global launch of generative search results and expanded their partnership with Reddit. This changed the way search surfaces user-generated content. Reddit threads are influencing search rankings more than ever and Google's AI Overviews prioritize UGC in search results.

For marketers, this opens up exciting possibilities.

As more Reddit content gets indexed by search engines, the platform has seen a noticeable uptick in top-of-funnel traffic and a corresponding rise in logged-in users. Brands can now show up in the SERP (in multiple languages) not only through their own domain but also through Reddit-related content. And if your brand or content resonates within those subreddits, you might snag a mention in an AI Overview. In other words: free social proof, directly in search.

CREATE ENGAGEMENT CONTENT FOR REDDIT

- cross-reference the SERP and keywords you want to rank for
- jump into existing Reddit conversations

- craft answers so good they earn upvotes
- foster authentic engagement
- track and revisit to refresh

The 4 Steps of the Community Growth Framework

In the following chapters, I'm going to dive deeper into the community growth framework and share examples of ways it's helped grow companies in real life. Here's what you can expect.

Step 1: Really Get to Know Your Customers

The foundation of community-driven growth is a deep, nuanced understanding of your customers that goes far beyond traditional demographic profiles or basic pain points. In Chapter 5, we'll explore how to develop what I call "living audience profiles"—dynamic, continuously evolving portraits of your customers as complete human beings.

This approach reveals not just what your customers need from your product, but how they think, where they spend time, who they trust, and what communities they already belong to. Unlike static buyer personas that sit unused in slide decks, living audience profiles become working tools that inform every marketing decision.

You'll learn how to:

- conduct research that uncovers hidden motivations and community connections;
- identify the spaces (both digital and physical) where your customers naturally gather;
- discover the shared language, values, and cultural references that unite your potential community;
- map existing relationships and networks you can tap into;
- recognize patterns that indicate readiness to engage with your community.

This deeper understanding sets the stage for everything that follows. When you truly know your customers—not as marketing targets but as potential community members—you create the conditions for authentic connection.

Step 2: Turn Knowledge into Resonance

With a rich understanding of your audience in place, the next step is transforming that knowledge into content, interactions, and experiences that genuinely resonate. In Chapter 6, we'll explore how to craft your brand's point of view and messaging in a way that connects emotionally with your audience.

The key insight here is that resonance happens at the intersection of your audience's reality and your unique perspective. It's not about shouting louder than competitors—it's about speaking more truthfully to what your audience actually experiences.

You'll discover how to:

- develop a distinctive brand POV that addresses your audience's challenges in a fresh way;
- identify the specific gaps between how your audience sees their problems and how they could see them;
- create content pillars that bridge your expertise with your audience's needs;
- design interaction models that feel natural to your target community members;
- balance educational value with emotional connection.

When your content and interactions resonate deeply, they create a magnetic pull that attracts your ideal community members. They recognize themselves in your message and feel understood in a way they don't elsewhere.

Step 3: Align Channel, Message, and Messenger

Even the most powerful message falls flat when delivered through the wrong channel or by the wrong voice. In Chapter 7, we'll explore how to create perfect alignment between where you show up, what you say, and who delivers your message.

This three-way alignment is what separates companies that build thriving communities from those that create content nobody engages with. When all three elements work together, your marketing feels less like marketing and more like a natural part of your audience's world.

You'll learn how to:

- identify which channels your audience already trusts and participates in;
- match content types to specific channels and audience mindsets;
- select the right messengers for different community segments;
- create authentic, multi-voice content strategies;
- develop channel-specific engagement approaches that feel native to each space.

The power of this alignment approach is that it respects how people naturally find and engage with communities. Instead of forcing your audience to adapt to your preferred channels and voices, you meet them where they are with messengers they can relate to.

Step 4: Create an Efficient Plan Using Media-First Supported by AI

The final step is implementing your community growth strategy efficiently. In Chapter 8, we'll explore how a media-first approach supported by AI allows you to create more impact with limited resources.

The traditional content creation model is unsustainable for most marketing teams. It leads to burnout, inconsistency, and diminishing returns as you struggle to maintain presence across multiple channels. The media-first approach flips this model on its head, starting with rich media assets that can be atomized across channels.

You'll discover how to:

- build a content production system around core media assets;
- use AI to efficiently expand, adapt, and distribute content;
- create balanced workflows that maintain quality while increasing output;
- design measurement systems that capture community growth indicators;
- build momentum through strategic content multiplication.

This approach allows you to show up consistently in multiple spaces without constantly creating new content from scratch. By starting with rich media and using AI as a multiplier, you can maintain an active presence across your community touchpoints without exhausting your team or budget.

When these four steps work together, they create a self-reinforcing system. Your deep customer knowledge informs resonant content delivered through aligned channels and messengers, all implemented efficiently through a media-first approach.

It's a cyclical framework—rather than a linear journey—that becomes more powerful with each iteration. As your community grows, you gain even deeper customer insights, which lead to more resonant content, better alignment, and more efficient production.

Trust the Process: Prioritizing Awareness and Affinity over Immediate Conversions

Brand affinity isn't built overnight. It takes time and repeated exposure to your message before customers form a connection strong enough to convert when they're ready. The same principles apply to internal influencers, who, over time, build trust and authenticity in their networks.

For businesses, this means acknowledging that investing in brand awareness won't always yield immediate, measurable ROI. But without it, the cost of conversion-focused strategies will only increase as competition becomes more intense.

REAL-WORLD EXAMPLE

Navattic's Influencer/Advisor Program

Navattic is a software platform that helps sales and marketing teams create interactive product demos.

One of the most impressive examples of community-driven growth I've seen comes from Navattic, who built an influencer/advisor program that demonstrates exactly how the community growth framework can deliver measurable results.

The program has been running for about two years. They started with just 2 influencers and now are up to 14. Here's the impact the program has had on growth:

LinkedIn Growth

- They recently hit 15k LinkedIn followers (added 10k in 1 year).

- Their head of marketing hit 10k LinkedIn followers (added 5k in 1 year).

Word of Mouth

- They grew word-of-mouth leads by 65 percent year-over-year.

- WOM is now their second-highest lead channel.

Quality Opportunities

- They have a 65 percent MQL to Opportunity rate (their strategy of education and data is helping bring in high-quality leads).

ROI

- ~1.8x ROI if looking at leads that come from mentioning an advisor or coming directly from LinkedIn.

- ~4x ROI if they add in WOM leads (which their advisors contribute to).

What makes this example so powerful is that it demonstrates the compounding effect of community-driven growth. The program didn't deliver these results in the first month or even the first quarter. It took consistent investment over time, but the results far exceeded what they could have achieved through traditional marketing approaches.

We Need to Talk About Crickets

Despite being a ubiquitous summer sound and source of relative calm, crickets aren't that friendly.

It turns out, they don't even meet their offspring. Once those baby cricket eggs are laid, mom and dad take off and leave their unborn babies to hatch and raise themselves.

And the males are *super* territorial and competitive, especially when it comes to mating. According to one study from the University of Exeter, male crickets who are five meters or more apart will chirp together in a kind of competitive chorus to create a louder siren song that attracts more females.[2]

Only this community virility song involves zero allegiances, friendship, or loyalty: If another male cricket is less than five meters away, he may go so far as to pick a fight with his neighbor to protect his chirping territory.

They're also surprisingly loud, making the common phrase, "it's crickets in here" somewhat of a paradox: Most crickets chirp at around 55–75 dB when heard from a few feet away, which on the high end is equivalent to a vacuum cleaner. And hearing a plural amount of crickets chirping in a competitive group lady call? It can be as loud as a busy restaurant.

Despite crickets being so independent that they abandon their offspring and fight with their neighbors, they still organically, genetically come together around one thing: mating with a female. In the cricket world, there's no leader, influencer, or even cultural pressure to kumbaya. The male crickets are intrinsically motivated to work together (but not too close together!) to increase their chances of achieving the outcome they all want. And when they do, they create a resonance that is exponential in its radius—ubiquitous, even, within the territory in which it reverberates.

It's a kind of strategic alliance where coming together and contributing their individual voices in the same place at the same time helps the whole group move from A to B, then it's every man for himself to close the deal.

From Crickets to Community

Interactions drive outcomes. One thing that motivates folks to interact is a shared interest or purpose. In the B2B world that usually takes the form of a tangible business outcome (not YOUR business outcome, your customers' business outcome). Therefore, building a community that organically facilitates interactions that drive outcomes will intrinsically motivate folks not only to join but also to engage regularly—and of their own accord—because they see the benefit of doing so without your help.

What I'm saying is the thesis for your community matters.

What I'm asking you is to stop making people busy; help them move forward.

What I'm telling you to do is to put away your megaphone; you don't need to talk loud when people are already gathered around you listening.

Conclusion: Communities Are the Future of B2B Growth

The B2B companies that will thrive in the coming years aren't those with the biggest advertising budgets or the most sophisticated martech stacks. They're the ones that build the most vibrant, engaged communities around their solutions.

Why? Because as traditional marketing channels become more saturated and expensive, community-driven growth offers an alternative that's both more effective and more sustainable. It leverages the fundamental human desire for connection and belonging while creating genuine business value.

This isn't just theory—it's happening all around us. Look at the most successful B2B companies in virtually any industry, and you'll find thriving communities at their center:

- Salesforce has built an empire on the back of its Trailblazer community.
- HubSpot's growth is powered by its academy, user groups, and partner ecosystem.
- Figma dominates design tools through its vibrant community of creators and plugins.

- Notion has exploded through template sharing and community-driven use cases.

The community growth framework I've outlined in this chapter gives you the structure to create similar results for your business, regardless of your size or resources. By really knowing your customers, turning that knowledge into resonant content, aligning channels and messengers, and implementing efficiently, you create the conditions for sustainable, compounding growth.

In the next chapter, we'll dive deeper into the first step of this framework: really getting to know your customers through living audience profiles. This foundation of deep customer understanding is what makes everything else possible.

Notes

1 Simmonds, R (2025) How to prepare for the rise of AIO & Reddit for SEO, Foundation Marketing, https://foundationinc.co/lab/aio-reddit-for-seo/ (archived at https://perma.cc/767E-B32L)

2 Morrison, A (2023) Male crickets court females in unison – unless rivals get too close, University of Exeter, https://news.exeter.ac.uk/faculty-of-health-and-life-sciences/male-crickets-court-females-in-unison-unless-rivals-get-too-close/ (archived at https://perma.cc/MDQ3-7RSU)

5

Getting to Really
Know Your Customers

What is curiosity? It is a desire to close some information gap that you notice. If you don't have that desire, you aren't curious by definition, period.

ROBERT MORTON, FOUNDER, HIGHLAND INSIGHTS

Marketing Mary Wants *More*

She's sick of being defined by categorical criteria. She is more than her job title and age. The company she works for? She likes it but it doesn't define her. It's merely a pitstop on this grand adventure she has planned in which she will transform multiple times, unearthing new thoughts, desires, fears, and expectations she can't even imagine right now.

Yet here she is, in her daily reductive stance, trapped in her prison cell of cubicle creativity trying to craft 3D comments for a 2D caricature of a human customer. She hears the digital swoosh as she shoots personality pixels across the internet and swears sometimes she can feel a microscopic breeze tussle her eyelashes as she Pac-Mans through her daydreaming about conversation, connection, and a turkey sandwich on the beach.

Despite her many attempts to make this known to B2B companies big and small, they continue to build their product—and marketing strategy—on broad-stroke personas that, frankly, she can't relate to.

How Did We Get Here?

Marketers have gotten so used to condensing complex human beings into demographic data and broad-strokes pain point that we began creating content solely for archetypes—not real people. And we move these digital mannequins along a made-up board game that we've played so many times that we know how the game will end from the first move. Which is fine because it gives us time to remember the before times when we didn't psychoanalyze search engines, social media was just a bunch of memes, Chat Roulette became a Ben Folds Five greatest hit, and Matt Bellassai got paid to get drunk at work and complain about it on camera once a week.

Those days are long since over and they've been replaced by a new internet that is even more fluid and enamored of forward motion. These days, the internet can only be defined by its constant evolution which, alongside the humans who build on it and hang out there, creates a pinball-like change experience that is occasionally cyclical, if "cyclical" looked like several timelines tripping and falling into each other like a bunch of toddlers who can't decide if they're mad, sad, happy, or, let's face it, sane.

This is the unpredictable baseline companies and marketers are working with when they try to carve their own path through the content jungle—then try to keep it clear long enough that people can find it. This fluidity demands marketing strategies that can adapt alongside the environment in which they're executed and the people they're intended to engage.

Simply put:

Traditional content marketing playbooks built around organic traffic from search, and brand-centric social and capture mechanisms like ebooks and white papers...

(to gate or not to gate, that has been a question that marketers have debated with a moral earnestness that implies, without evidence, that actual human beings have been harmed in the execution of one or the other)

...no longer support how modern buyers make decisions.

The problem is no longer that we lack data about our customers. Most B2B companies are drowning in it. We have demographics, firmographics, technographics, and every other graphic you can imagine. We track their every digital move. We survey them constantly.

Yet despite all the data available, most companies still don't really know their customers.

They think they do, but their marketing suggests otherwise. And while much of that is explained by the pressures of startup funding or the gluttonous growth expectations of the street, the fact is, even companies that are trying still don't understand what truly influences their customers' decisions, what keeps them up at night, or what makes them trust one solution over another.

When companies and their marketers don't understand—and embrace—the nuances of their customers they end up creating noise, not content, and the impact it has on their success is decisive:

- Their product is a configuration of features and price, entering it into a bottom-feeding competition that creates the perception that their product is disposable.
- CAC is higher—avoidably so.
- Growth becomes an exercise in brute force volume of activities, causing an inefficient cycle of "throw more money at it" merely because the company can't quantitatively measure the impact of things like word of mouth, a free and higher-converting form of marketing derived from things like brand affinity, which are like curse words to many B2B leaders.

The good news is there's a way through this valley of gloom. I'm going to show you how you can build or join communities without being constrained by rigid playbooks. Instead, you'll attract folks in the community by being yourself. And in so doing, you will attract folks to your product—and you—through authentic engagement and encourage others to do the same.

You'll learn how to:

- discover complex insights about your customers rather than checking data boxes;

- learn what's really on their mind, not just what they say matters;
- identify the community spaces (both digital and physical) where your customers naturally gather;
- build living customer profiles and how to interact with them to get more useful information to guide your content strategy.

But first, it's time to check in on your customers.

B2B Buyers, Decision-Makers, and Leaders Are Changing

There is a new group of B2B buyers entering the market and the companies that are excited to capitalize on this opportunity will win.

These buyers are more diverse, in more ways, than ever before. And the revenue opportunity is staggering for companies that are paying attention.

I'm not just talking about present-day circumstances. I'm looking at a not-too-distant future where the B2B buyer market is going to look, behave, and make decisions much differently than they do today:

- **They don't care about your tech.** They take it for granted because they grew up with it, making you virtually (pun!) invisible to them. Because of this, buyers are becoming even more discerning and keenly attuned to real value versus representative value.

- **They reject your paradigm.** The next generation of decision-makers may be influenced by the generation before but certainly aren't going to behave like we did. The way they make decisions and what they consider substantive will be unrecognizable to folks who cling to reboots and old-world thinking.

- **They don't want you just because you're popular.** Next gen buyers experience community and build trust with others through their fierce individuality. They like to get in the weeds and debate. They find community by being themselves to attract other like-minded folks.

Combined with their upbringing with tech as table stakes, they are more "micro-opinionated" and therefore more nuanced in their decision-making criteria. One single brand message may not rule them all anymore.

This is, in part, the result of a few macroeconomic and cultural changes, which I will illustrate using recent population data in the United States as a proxy.

Leadership Teams Are (Very) Slowly Showing Signs That Someday They Might Become Less Homogeneous

Here's where we're at.

Buying committees are bigger: According to Forrester's 2024 Buyers' Journey Survey, the average number of people on B2B buying committees is up to 13.[1]

Decision-makers are steadily—albeit slowly—becoming more diverse. According to the Census Bureau the total US population grew by 14 percent between 2004 and 2022, showing growth across a range of ethnic groups:[2]

- Asian population grew 74%
- Hispanic population grew 55%
- Black populations grew 22%

Meanwhile, the white population remained stable, resulting in an overall drop in the white American population from 65 percent in 2004 to 59 percent in 2022.[3]

Unfortunately, increased diversity in population does not result equitably in diversity among leadership, and it's for illogical, unfair reasons. However, I believe that the gap is going to continue shrinking and this is going to be a positive change for companies and marketers alike, so hear me out.

Looking at the 2023 US Bureau of Labor Statistics (BLS) annual data (reported in January 2024), Black or African American workers held 9.2 percent of management occupations in the United States.[4] While this percentage reflects race-based inequity that is still unacceptably high, what is significant about it is the uptick in pace: In the previous 10-year period, from 2012 to 2022, the share of Black or African American workers in management increased from 7.3 percent to 8.9 percent.[5] While still underrepresented, women now occupy 28 percent of C-suite positions in North America (up from 17 percent a decade ago), according to McKinsey's Women in the Workplace 2023 report.[6]

Based solely on ongoing population trends, these groups are destined to continue occupying more leadership roles and influencing how buying decisions are made at their companies. For example, research from CEB (now Gartner)[7] shows that when women are involved in B2B purchase decisions, they place greater emphasis on:

1 comprehensive research across multiple channels

2 seeking diverse perspectives

3 sharing useful content with colleagues

4 evaluating long-term relationship potential with vendors

But buying criteria isn't the only or the most significant change that will impact marketing teams and the economy. Two things are about to converge that stand to have a positive impact not just on the economy, but also on how companies sell.

First, the great wealth transfer is underway: Women, who currently manage approximately $31.8 trillion of global spending, are expected to control 75 percent of discretionary spending worldwide in the next five years due to generational wealth reallocation from Baby Boomers to Millennials.[8] This is paired with data showing that companies with a greater representation of women and ethnically diverse executive teams are 39 percent more likely to financially outperform those that don't.[9] With more money changing hands to folks who are statistically more likely to do a better job using it, who knows what types of opportunities lie ahead?

What Does Increased Diversity in Buyers' Control of Wealth Mean for B2B Content Marketing?

CONTENT STRATEGY THAT ASSUMES A MONOLITHIC AUDIENCE WILL UNDERPERFORM

For B2B content marketers, these changes demand a reassessment of their strategic approach, which may unconsciously cater to traditionally male-dominated buying committees.

Pretty soon, you'll be building relationships with buyers, decision-makers, and leadership teams who have a broader range of backgrounds, values, and perspectives among them.

This is where your opportunity lies.

While a lot of companies have been laser focused on AI, the truly disruptive opportunity is slowly revealing itself, and very few are paying attention or preparing to capitalize on it. My bet: the companies—and marketers—that are prepared to serve this next generation of decision-makers will win bigger than the ones who are obsessing over AI efficiency. This is a unique advantage available for the taking.

GAINING CUSTOMERS' TRUST IS MORE NUANCED THAN EVER

Countless studies have has shown that customer trust and loyalty have a direct impact on a company's bottom line. And it isn't just in net new sales or retention. PWC published a report in 2024 that showed 46 percent of customers spent more and 28 percent paid a premium at companies they trust.[10] The biggest impact finding was from word of mouth: 61 percent have recommended a company they trust to friends or family.[11]

According to Edelman's 2024 Trust Barometer, consumers named trust in the brand "important" or a "deal breaker" when making purchase decisions—holding the #3 spot for a second consecutive year.[12] They also saw a new deciding factor shoot up five points year-over-year to #8 (entering the top 10 for the first time): "I trust the company that owns the brand."[13]

There is a big brand affinity opportunity here against your competitors, because while 90 percent of executives believe customers highly trust their companies, only 30 percent of customers actually do, according to a study by PWC.[14]

What Does All This Mean for Customer Research?

While larger, more diverse buying committees present an new opportunity, one thing remains the same: Generally speaking, people are not that self-aware, so asking them to articulate their true motivations often tells you something completely different from what they actually said.

Surveys are only useful for simple questions. I see them more as preventative tools. They prevent you from making avoidable mistakes before launching an experiment or narrowing down the possible causes of something you're trying to solve, mostly just to save time.

The current state of marketing research typically falls into two patterns:

1 teams have quantitative data but struggle to derive meaningful insights or reach consensus on its interpretation;
2 they have customer research but aren't acting on it effectively.

What This Means for Your Content Strategy

Your content strategy must adapt to connect with more diverse decision-making committees. To do that, you need to understand not just the individuals on the committee but also the dynamics between them. Who has influence and who doesn't? Who wishes they were in charge and shows it? This will vary dramatically by industry, company, leadership, money, emotions, and so many more factors, as with most things that involve humans. In other words: *It depends.*

> *Your content strategy must adapt to connect with more diverse decision-making committees.*

Your job is to fill in the blanks of what it depends on. The good news: Participating in the community will organically surface a lot of this knowledge. But for those inevitable times when you have to go after it, here are some things that have worked for me.

How I Conduct Customer Research Like a Human Person

To me, learning about people is an infinite and not a finite game. The whole point of it is to keep playing so you can deepen the relationship, build trust, and be there at the beginning of change, so you're more prepared for it.

When you are immersed in the community you serve, a lot of the time the information presents itself to you organically. All you have to do is listen and connect the dots.

That said, seeking information is a good idea too. Here are some things I've done that yielded a ton of information, relationships, partnerships, and ultimately value for customers and the company I worked for (in no particular order and without prescribed method).

Don't Be a Wallflower

This is why the community growth framework works. Everything is integrated and therefore efficient. Your research isn't separate from customer engagement, awareness, etc.

If you're not curious about your customers, you won't come up with good ideas, because you'll always be looking for a shortcut to understanding. That usually manifests as some kind of programmatic data collection or some other hack that returns only empirical answers with no color.

Active participation in customer communities (both yours and existing professional communities) provides constant learning opportunities. Pay attention to:

- questions they ask each other
- resources they share
- language they use
- challenges they discuss

Your customers don't stop being human beings when they're at work. They have emotions, biases, and personal motivations that influence their professional decisions. Understanding these human elements is crucial for creating resonant content.

Forget all that social listening, sales call shadowing. Forget the structure and participate in the community! Interact with customers online, offline, wherever they hang out. Introduce yourself, explain why you're there, be human, not just as a brand representative. Doing so will create an environment where folks feel open to sharing their real challenges and frustrations.

THE INTERVIEW MAP METHOD
Hannah Shamji, *Customer Researcher for B2B SaaS*

Define the decision your research will inform

Say you want to understand customer pain points. Great, but for what? A homepage rewrite? A sales email? A pricing page? The level of detail you need depends on your goal. A homepage might require broad emotional triggers, while a sales email needs sharp, specific objectives. If you don't define the business decision you're trying to inform, you risk collecting insights that feel useful but don't translate into action.

Pinpoint what you want to learn (down to the details)

Don't settle for just "pain points." Be more specific: Pain points around what? Are you investigating frustrations with their current process? Barriers to switching? Problems they had with their last solution? The more specific your pursuit, the more useful your insights will be.

Talk to sales, support, and frontline staff to fill in the gaps

Your frontline teams hear patterns every day. Maybe sales knows people hesitate because they assume setup will take weeks. Maybe support keeps hearing confusion about a key feature. Instead of starting from zero, use their knowledge to refine your questions. For example, if setup time keeps coming up, you don't need to confirm it's an issue, you can cut straight to: "I've heard setup is a challenge. Was it for you? What happened?" This lets you go deeper, faster.

Identify what's still missing/unknown

Maybe every team agrees that price is a concern, but is that the real issue or just the most visible one? While sales hears "price," product hears "missing features," and support hears "steep learning curve." Now you have conflicting signals, and an opening to dig deeper. The point of this step isn't to validate all those signals—it's to determine where to focus. These questions will help you get there:

- Where are the obvious gaps—the ones everyone acknowledges?

- What details are still fuzzy or incomplete (even after talking to frontline teams)?

- What parts of the customer journey are total mysteries (or not even on the team's radar)?

Draft starter questions and question angles

This is where the Interview Map comes in handy. It gets you to what I call Level 1 data—the first answer the customer gives you. That's your starting point. For every question I follow up with at least five or six more. That's when you start to get to the most useful feedback. Now cross-check your map against the five Ws:

- Who's involved?

- What's happening?

- When does it occur?

- Where does it happen?

- Why does it unfold this way?

By cross-checking your map against the 5 Ws, you'll zero in on the details that matter, identify what doesn't need further discovery, and head into your calls with a clear sense of focus.

There's No "Way" to Do Customer Research

While I do typically have something I want to learn, I don't use a method when I talk to customers. This wasn't a strategic choice, if I'm being honest. It was just a "way" that felt natural to me and got folks to open up.

My general approach is to make it feel informal, make them laugh, and ask off-the-cuff questions to demonstrate genuine interest instead of checking boxes. My goal is to make them relaxed to reveal any unspoken context from things like tone and body language. Best case scenario: They trust me enough to share context that can't be shared but that reveals something helpful I can work with. Here are some of my go-to tactics for interviews. Again, this is not a method, it's just things that yielded good insights for me over the years:

WASTE TIME
Do this at the beginning of the interview to set a more informal tone. Don't ask them about their weekend, though. Ask them what their morning routine is or the last concert they went to.

DON'T MAKE ASSUMPTIONS
Wherever you find yourself connecting dots in your head, share the story with them and ask, "What is your reaction to this?"

> *Listen to what they say.*

Seriously, stop looking at Slack and listen. If you're struggling to identify follow-up questions then you're not listening and you're making assumptions.

If you are listening and you have that feeling like there's something you haven't uncovered, throw in something random, and don't give any context. One question that surprises folks and gets them talking is, "What do you hate?" It doesn't have to be about the product, but don't tell them that. Just ask the question and let them answer based on how they interpret it.

I find this question doesn't lead to negative conversation loops. Instead, it encourages them to think out loud and even become more positive. This one is hard to explain, so just try it. And don't let them get away with not answering.

WHAT WOULD YOU LIKE?
I learned this question from my CEO coach, Cecilia Montalbano. After a "woe is me" rant, she'd say, "Ok, so what would you like instead?" The question snapped me out of whatever negative loop I

was in and forced me to consider the alternative. Another thing she did that really annoyed me in the beginning but also totally worked: She stayed silent until I found an answer even if it took me a while.

Just in case my no "way" way doesn't work for you (fair), here is another customer interview method by Robert Morton, founder, Highland Insights, and board member with over 20 years in senior marketing roles at Blackboard, Motley Fool and others.

HUMAN-CENTERED GROWTH INQUIRY

Robert Morton, *Founder, Highland Insights*

Organizations often make customer research more complicated than it has to be, because they fear they can't learn anything without a massive effort. That mindset just leads to inaction. My approach:

Just start conversing.

You'll gather actionable information almost immediately, and the gains will compound quickly. To get started all you need is one question. It doesn't really matter what the question is as long as it's something you're actively curious about and will help you do something differently in the short run.

These are a few questions that have worked for me:

- Who really are our most valuable customers and what makes that true?

- Why do customers turn to us in the first place?

- What progress are they looking to make, whether we exist or not?

- What makes customers leave (how do I keep them from wanting to)?

- What makes a good customer? A less good one?

- How does this specific customer segment use our product and what for?

- How do customers think about this specific feature?

- Would we retain customers better if we did x or y?

- What's encouraging/discouraging a repeat purchase?

CONVERSATIONAL INQUIRY

This is an open-ended approach that can be challenging for marketers to execute because they often feel pressured to validate specific hypotheses or gather feedback on product features during interviews. There's nothing wrong with that inherently, but it's essentially confirming a story you already have. This confirmatory bent leads to inquiries that tend that yield limited value, or at least limited insights.

Try instead to approach the interview without steering the conversation to a specific outcome or "right" answer. Instead, hold the wheel of the conversation more lightly, take side roads and go where the conversation takes you. You're more likely to uncover things like identifying an unexpected competitive advantage or learning that customers prefer a simpler solution than what you planned to build.

Finally, I recommend recording your interviews and reviewing them at a later date. The most valuable and surprising insights often emerge when marketers can dig into the conversations they had both in the moment and afterwards with a little distance.

Creating a Living Customer Profile with AI

Customer research shouldn't be a one-time project.

Neither should your customer profiles. Remember Marketing Mary? Yeah, those profiles always annoyed her. The world she lives in is changing constantly, which means that even the pic you snapped of her two years ago is outdated (those heart sunglasses she wore everywhere, *ugh*).

The reality is that there are often multiple departments doing their own customer research simultaneously, but they aren't always coordinating their efforts or sharing knowledge. This is inefficient and often leads to factions within the company coming to varying conclusions about your customer.

A centralized customer knowledge base that folks across departments can contribute to is a living source of truth that's more comprehensive and thus more likely to lead to new, unique ideas. It also helps remove some of the silos between departments that plague many B2B companies.

Instead of dusty tomes, your customer profiles become more like ongoing relationships that continuously yield new information that you can use in your content strategy (and other departments, too). Living audience profiles are conversational, current, and better reflect the humans they represent. Plus, with the various ways AI enables you to interact with that knowledge, you can imagine how even basic things like headline generation or topic brainstorms come first from customers and not keywords.

The Ongoing Journey

Really knowing your customers isn't a destination—it's a continuous journey of discovery and adjustment. The market changes. Customers' needs evolve. New challenges emerge. Your understanding must keep pace:

- Stop worrying about how to do customer research and just start talking to them.
- Prepare for customer interviews.
- There is no one "way" to talk to customers. Just go into each conversation with a desire to learn, listen to what they say, and dig deeper with questions.
- Don't be afraid to pause. Silence is so uncomfortable to most people that it almost always gets them to talk.

The good news? Each step toward deeper customer understanding makes your content marketing more effective. Every insight helps you create content that truly resonates with your audience. Every learning cycle brings you closer to your customers.

Conclusion: The Ongoing Journey of Customer Understanding

Really knowing your customers isn't a destination you arrive at once—it's a continuous journey that evolves as rapidly as the market itself. The B2B landscape changes. Customer needs shift. New challenges emerge. Decision-making committees grow more diverse. Your understanding must keep pace.

This journey requires sustained curiosity—that genuine desire to close information gaps that Robert Morton describes. Without true curiosity driving your customer research, you'll keep recycling the same insights and missing the deeper truths that drive decisions.

The most important takeaways for truly knowing your customers:

Start with genuine conversation, not rigid methodology. Frameworks can guide you, but shouldn't constrain you. The best insights often come from letting conversations flow naturally, staying silent when necessary, and asking unexpected questions that reveal hidden motivations.

Participate actively in the community. Don't just observe from a distance. Jump in, introduce yourself, share knowledge, and build relationships. The richest customer insights come through direct engagement, not passive observation.

Create living customer profiles. Static personas are dead on arrival. Instead, build dynamic knowledge systems that evolve with your customers and integrate insights from across your organization. AI makes this more accessible than ever before.

Recognize diversity as opportunity. The growing diversity in B2B buying committees isn't just a demographic shift—it's a strategic advantage for companies prepared to understand these evolving perspectives. Those who prepare now will have a significant edge as these changes accelerate.

Trust is increasingly complex but critically important. In an environment where only 30 percent of customers actually trust the companies they do business with, authentic understanding creates a genuine competitive advantage.

Each step toward deeper customer understanding makes your content marketing exponentially more effective. Every insight helps you create content that truly resonates with your audience.

Every learning cycle brings you closer to the people making decisions.

In the next chapter, we'll explore how to transform this deep customer understanding into content that genuinely resonates—creating the kind of magnetic pull that attracts your ideal audience and builds lasting relationships.

Notes

1 Hawthorne, A (2025) The verdict is in: It's buying groups for the Win, Forrester, www.forrester.com/blogs/the-verdict-is-in-its-buying-groups-for-the-win/ (archived at https://perma.cc/ZVZ5-CV3E)

2 U.S. Census Bureau (2024) National population totals and components of change: 2020-2024, Census.gov,: www.census.gov/data/tables/time-series/demo/popest/2020s-national-total.html#v2024 (archived at https://perma.cc/2V4W-LCG2)

3 Hatfield, J (2024) How U.S. public opinion has changed in 20 years of our surveys, Pew Research Center, www.pewresearch.org/2024/09/13/how-us-public-opinion-has-changed-in-20-years-of-our-surveys/#fn-187129-1 (archived at https://perma.cc/E55U-FNH3)

4 U.S. Bureau Of Labor Statistics (2024) Current Population Survey (CPS), Bls.gov, www.bls.gov/cps/ (archived at https://perma.cc/VG9K-JXKB)

5 Ibid.

6 McKinsey & Company (2024) Women in the workplace, www.mckinsey.com/featured-insights/diversity-and-inclusion/women-in-the-workplace (archived at https://perma.cc/65E2-BADW)

7 Gartner (2024) Gartner survey finds women represent 31 percent of senior-level B2B sales employees despite making up nearly half of the global workforce, www.gartner.com/en/newsroom/press-releases/2024-03-05-gartner-survey-finds-women-represent-thirty-one-percent-of-senior-level-b2b-sales-employees-despite-making-up-nearly-half-of-the-global-workforce (archived at https://perma.cc/7TH7-CZB7)

8 Graham, K (2024) Shaping success: A deep dive into women's impact on the CPG landscape, NIQ, https://nielseniq.com/global/en/insights/analysis/2024/shaping-success-a-deep-dive-into-womens-impact-on-the-cpg-landscape/ (archived at https://perma.cc/HQ5N-XF8S)

9 McKinsey & Company (2023) Diversity matters even more: the case for holistic impact, McKinsey & Company, www.mckinsey.com/featured-insights/diversity-and-inclusion/diversity-matters-even-more-the-case-for-holistic-impact (archived at https://perma.cc/M6LU-C3JM)

10 PwC (2024) Trust in US Business Survey, www.pwc.com/us/en/library/trust-in-business-survey.html (archived at https://perma.cc/FPZ4-3VVS)

11 Ibid.

12 Edelman (2024) 2024 Edelman Trust Barometer, www.edelman.com/trust/2024/trust-barometer (archived at https://perma.cc/9R2L-CVZY)

13 Ibid.

14 PwC (2024) Trust in US Business Survey, www.pwc.com/us/en/library/trust-in-business-survey.html (archived at https://perma.cc/2PVV-QU5C)

6

Turning Knowledge into Resonance

You can't have ROI without the joy.

ANN HANDLEY

This is going to be hard to explain.

It all started at a marketing conference that took place at a hotel across the street from my apartment in Brooklyn.

My friends and I arrived the first morning a tad bleary eyed after the pre-party I'd hosted on my roof the night before. But we were excited to be there, because a bunch of our marketing friends from all over had flown in to speak and attend.

I'd (obviously) been to the hotel several times already for rooftop parties and dinner at the Italian restaurant, but when we walked into the lobby, I realized I had no idea where to go. I'd never attended a conference there before.

Almost immediately, we recognized friendly faces across the hall on a kind of mezzanine half-circle space with two staircases leading to the basement wrapped around either side. As we started down the left staircase, we hit an unexpected traffic jam. Standing on the stairs was someone who looked like a celebrity surrounded by what appeared to be paparazzi. These "photographers" blocked our path as the "celebrity" posed and prepared to descend.

Suddenly, the paparazzi erupted into action, clamoring over each other, yelling questions like "Hey, over here!" Camera flashes burst through the space as the celebrity walked down toward the conference area. Total chaos unfolded all around us, as conference-goers exchanged puzzled looks as the paparazzi bumped into them, scrambling to get a picture of this guy we'd never heard of.

When we finally made it down the stairs we spotted friends and asked what was going on. Meanwhile, these paparazzi guys kept bumping into us as they scrambled.

I initially assumed they were filming background for a movie because they shoot in my neighborhood at least weekly, and there were production trucks parked nearby. But when I shared this theory with my friend Ryan, he replied, "No, somebody hired them. It's like a TikTok thing. Someone hired them to make a big deal about them at the conference."

I was skeptical, but these photographers kept following the same man and woman around, both dressed impeccably. It was annoying given the tight quarters, but not a huge issue.

Later, when I noticed the photographers taking a break, I seized my opportunity. I approached them, so confused I didn't even know what to ask. They were wearing tuxedos, which already signaled they weren't authentic paparazzi. By then, I'd concluded that Audience Plus must have hired them as part of their post-conference content strategy.

"What are you doing here?" I asked them directly.

They stayed in character: "We're paparazzi!" One flashed a press pass at me, while another pulled out a tiny $100 bill the size of a piece of gum, saying, "Look, I made money!"

Eventually, they gave me a knowing wink and nod, but I still wasn't satisfied. The whole thing was confounding to me and most of the other conference attendees. What were we supposed to DO with the experience? And who did they represent?

It turned out Apollo had brought the fake paparazzi as some kind of immersive installation. I found out at lunch from a friend of mine who, it just so happened, had just accepted a job there. If it weren't for her, I'm not sure I would have known what company they were promoting since they weren't wearing any company swag and the only reason they spoke to me was because I cornered them on a break.

Even though it was weird and kind of annoying—anti-resonant, if you will—they were the buzz of the conference as we all tried to figure out what the heck was going on and then gossiped about how strange it was after. I even told the story on my podcast!

What Is Resonance?

Most things in life aren't interesting on their own. Messages, stories, pictures, videos—they all need something in them that the person consuming them can relate to strongly enough that they're intrinsically motivated to continue engaging or act.

Which means the messenger alone isn't enough. That's because resonance consists of three things coming together that form a bond with your customer (Figure 6.1).

Think of your favorite comedian testing new material—even the most experienced and popular comedians in the world will sometimes hear crickets from the audience. That's because of context. It's just about not the teller—even a famous comedian can't save a joke that the audience doesn't relate to.

FIGURE 6.1 Resonance Framework

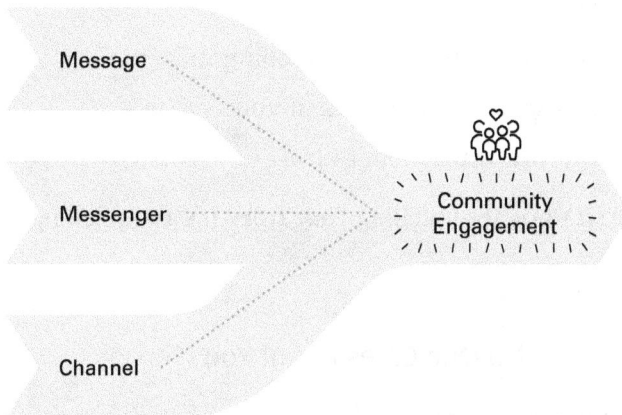

Message

Messenger

Community Engagement

Channel

> "Audiences aren't actively seeking your brand's content. They're looking for connection."
>
> **Rachel Downey**, CEO, Share Your Genius

A story is interesting when:

- You tell the story to people who can relate in some way (it's being told *for* your audience not *to* them).

- You summarize the context, going into detail where it deepens the plot, surprises your audience, makes them laugh, etc.

- You organize information into a logical order to achieve the reaction you want from your audience. (Logical doesn't mean chronological; logical represents any structure that creates both surprise and clarity. This is a taste thing, so enjoy the trial and error!)

- It's got *style* baby. The vibe of story, your tone and cadence, word choices—they are part of the world you're creating. When you tailor the vibe to your audience, paint background elements they will notice while leaving the rest fuzzy.

Make sure you're connecting necessary dots and sharing enough detail to help customers:

- understand what you're trying to communicate

- experience a sense of belonging in your vision

- feel the way you want them to feel

Remember: It's not about telling *your* story, it's about telling *their* story.

No One Cares About You (Sorry)

Remember when you were a little kid, and you created "works of art" by gluing dried pasta onto construction paper? You'd proudly hand your masterpiece to your parents, who would squeal with delight: "WOW! That's AMAZING!" Your heart would swell with pride as they hung it on the fridge, your illegible signature a testament to your creative genius.

Well, I've got some bad news: That part of your life is over.

As an adult, you discover that mom and dad threw out your macaroni art two weeks after they hung it up. And by the time you've entered the job market, that's when it really sinks in:

No one cares about you.

It's true! They don't care about your LinkedIn post, that video you shared (yes, even though it got a lot of likes), your marketing plan, or that email you spent three hours perfecting. Oh, and they don't care about your new job either—they said congratulations on LinkedIn because it prompted them to and they wanted other people to see so they commented too.

Now, here's the part that keeps your CEO up at night: No one, not one single person, *cares about their product.*

Especially journalists. It's true. The original fake news is every press release sent by B2B SaaS companies about their latest product launch. And even if they did care (which again, they definitely don't), the people who read that nerdy news don't need convincing so it's not worth the PR money you paid to get written about.

Oh and one more thing—the thing they really, *really* don't care about? Whatever it is you want from them.

Harsh? I disagree.

This is a motivating reality to growth-minded folks. It ignites their creative spark and gets them out of bed in the morning. It's the taunting whisper between their ears that inspires them to create resonant content that inspires the community in which you are operating to fall in love with your brand and, for those who are ready, to be excited to purchase your product.

According to the Content Marketing Institute's 2024 research, 82 percent of top-performing B2B companies attribute their success primarily to "understanding their audience." Yet in the same study, 55 percent of B2B marketers cited challenges with "creating content that prompts desired action."[1]

This is the resonance gap. It's the black hole between what you *think* you understand about your customers and what you truly do. This chasm of blindness tricks you into believing that your siren song is a free will manifestation.

What's worse, you are mistaking what is most often circumstance with actual resonance, not realizing that you were chosen by procurement, your founders, the buying committee, or more likely budget.

The good news? People *want* to care. And it's that secret desire that we marketers spend our careers trying to capture.

Why No One Cares About You

Most of the time, when your marketing doesn't resonate, the thing that happens is *nothing*.

Not that this is any consolation, because silence is the most dangerous thing in the world to a business trying to grow—even worse than negative attention (at least then they know you exist!).

The silence is what you should fear the most, because it's like a megaphone that no one cares about you enough to even tell you it sucks (or your reach is so low that no one saw it). If you're replacing customer immersion with community participation, there's almost no way the fearsome silence will ever occur. You won't just know too much, you'll have a community of like-minded individuals to check with before you go out with it in the first place.

When I worked in customer support, I learned that the angry customers are not the ones you have to worry about. They're still invested if they took the time to tell you they're having a problem. It's the ones that just leave that you need to worry about. The ones that see you as so disposable that they simply delete their account and forget all about you.

Ever have to listen to someone tell a story that they inserted into the conversation even though it didn't really fit? Or at conferences when someone inelegantly steers a group conversation in a direction so they can talk about themselves? That is what it's like when your marketing doesn't resonate. No one is coming at you with pitchforks, blasting you for being boring. It's so much worse than that: They'll just stop thinking about you altogether.

Most B2B Content Fails to Resonate for Three Reasons

There are three primary buckets of resonance failure that I've observed in my career:

- **Focused on output over impact**
  Companies obsess over production metrics (how many blog posts, social posts, or emails they create) rather than resonance metrics (how their content changes audience behavior or perception).

- **Mistaking information for insight**
  They share what they know rather than what their audience wants or needs to learn.

- **Broadcasting instead of connecting**
  They treat content as a megaphone for their message rather than a bridge to their audience. According to CMI's research, 61 percent of B2B organizations cite it as a challenge to successfully create content that appeals to different stages of the buyer's journey.[2]

But just naming them isn't enough. To avoid these mistakes, it's more helpful to understand the reasons behind those mistakes. This is a list of mistakes I've observed in my career, some of which I have made myself:

- you're not paying attention so you mistake surface-level understanding for deep understanding;
- you're sharing something (a message, post, etc.) because *you* want to share it, not because your customers care;
- your CEO suggested it;
- you want a person or group of people to know something about you, so you force it into the conversation (similar to the above scenario, but involves even less self-awareness);

- you think you're self-aware but you're not, so you're not listening;
- you care about the story so much that you believe it's more interesting to more people than it actually is (probably because you're not a good listener);
- you indulge in too many details (see bullet above).

Noticing a theme? YOU. You are the problem. It's not that you yourself aren't interesting, it's that you're sharing something because you care about it and not because anyone else wants to hear it. Or the way you're telling the story is boring, so the people who would otherwise be interested miss the message.

That's right, dear reader, we're talking subjectivity. The good and evil perched on opposite shoulders pulling the self-awareness strings that lead you to success or failure. And you're right, it feels like you're doomed to fail, because *how would you even know if you're self-aware or not?*

This is again where community participation saves the day. When you develop genuine relationships with your customers, you allow them to occupy more of your mindshare (and push YOU out). Then a new principle will naturally emerge:

> *Just because you think something is good doesn't mean other people will, too.*

It may sound like a *duh* thing to say, but this is a mindset for me that keeps me from falling in love with my own ideas. The problem with getting really good at what you do is that your deepened knowledge and elevated taste can make your ideas less resonant if you don't adopt this humbly objective mindset.

You Don't Know What You're Saying

Marketers love their marketing terms. Right now, you are trapped by one of my personal favorites: resonance. Trust me: I'm annoyed at myself too. Our obsession with jargon has led to a lot of meaningless words being used to represent actual knowledge and understanding. In reality, these terms we use are highly interpretable and lead to a lot of the disappointment, misunderstanding, and perception of poor execution/quality that marketers experience with their CEO, product leaders, and even folks on their own team. Terms like:

- know your customer
- understand your customer
- resonate
- engage
- amplify
- connect
- drive action

Stop right now and write down your definitions of these terms as they relate to marketing. Now share with the rest of your marketing team, your CMO, your CEO. Do you all understand them the exact same way? Probably not, and it matters, because if you're doing marketing designed to achieve any of these outcomes or deploying them as actions, then you're more likely to miss.

This isn't semantics, it's strategy. Because when you define these terms (or use more applicable words) for your company, your marketing, your customer, you're creating a foundation that ensures alignment with the many people involved, thus gaining a greater chance that you'll succeed in achieving the outcomes you want.

These words and phrases are inherently unhelpful, because none of them explain how "knowing" or "resonating" actually manifest. They hold no globally applicable meaning. A company could say they know their customer because they did market research, conducted surveys and customer interviews, analyzed behavioral trends in the product, conducted competitor research, then created customer personas like Marketing Mary. But we've already established that data and demographics alone don't equal knowing.

How Do You Make People Care About You?

In a sea of sameness, you are all you've got.

Knowledge is a commodity. Facts are commodities. *Content* is a commodity—and B2B companies keep churning out more and more. With all that competition, commodity content, and copycatting, does a resonant hum even exist that no one has ever heard before?

When I was Director of Content at Help Scout, competitors copied us all the time. When we published a blog post, we knew the next day an almost identical version would be published by one of our competitors. We didn't care. What made our content unique wasn't just words on a page, it was our founding principles which the company upheld and reflected vigorously. It was the combination of unique brains executing together and embracing Help Scout's guiding principles. There was a distinct feeling when you engaged with anything Help Scout, and that could not be copied.

You are the only you that exists in the world. No one else has your exact experiences, thoughts, etc. Thus, out of the gate, you are unique. Thus, you have something unique to offer. The same is true of your product or company.

"What you know matters. But what you say and how you say it determines whether other people care."

Jay Acunzo, author/host of *How Stories Happen*

I know what you're thinking and you're wrong: Even copycats can't capture you. They can make your exact technology, they can copy your exact marketing tactics, but no one else can create your vibe, your essence—the things that really attract people to you.

While your uniqueness is the secret ingredient, that alone won't make people care. It needs other ingredients to make it work for your business. Fajr Muhammad, VP of Content Strategy and Growth at iPullRank, describes this as Resonance Design.

> RESONANCE DESIGN
>
> **Fajr Muhammad**, *VP of Content Strategy and Growth at iPullRank*
>
> Data reveals how long a visitor stays and what they did after they landed, but digital marketing channels and content are increasingly about how a user *feels* about their experience. Where content used to be about authority and experience, it's now about adding up the sum of its parts to drive resonance:
>
> - **SEO** tells you what terms people are searching and how to structure your page.
> - **Content strategy** outlines how this launch fits into your broader narrative, what channels to use, and what story to tell.
> - **Design** ensures that the journey is frictionless and visually appealing.
>
> Add them all up and Resonance Design ensures that when someone lands on your site, they're led through a journey that feels natural, delightful, and deeply resonates with them.

Forget "Thought Leadership" and Be Vulnerable

"Thought leadership," when content marketers first began using it, was intended to differentiate their company by surfacing the unique thoughts of their founders, executives, and experts.

It's always been difficult to execute on, namely because executives are understandably busy and it's hard to fake knowledge you don't have. There are two common reasons why this happens:

- marketer doesn't know enough about the topic to effectively express the nuances of the thought;
- leader boils down their thought (or edits the meaty parts out) because they think that's what marketing wants or because they're afraid to share what they really think.

I've been the marketer writing for my CEO trying to represent knowledge I didn't have *and* the leader who was afraid to share my thoughts and ideas.

I remember when I was a CEO I shared a LinkedIn post that was extremely vulnerable and therefore felt risky to share given my position. Looking back, though, it was a classic example of turning knowledge into resonance.

Many folks had privately shared their own vulnerabilities with me related to work since I became a CEO and asked my advice—most of them women. They were grateful when I shared my own challenges and vulnerabilities with them and said so in LinkedIn DMs, emails, and texts. I didn't have official data, but I was listening to the community, and I knew their struggles and wishes.

Having all this knowledge about my community, I made an educated guess that seeing a woman in an executive position be vulnerable publicly would demonstrate bravery and show them they were not alone.

Here's what I posted:

I feel deep personal shame every time I make a mistake.

One reason I've "succeeded" in my career is because I'm so deeply afraid of disappointing people that I avoid making mistakes at all costs.

When I really mess up, I deprive myself of things that bring me joy, because I don't think I deserve happiness.

I've been told I'm unusually self-aware, but that's just fear masquerading as an asset. My need to please other people makes me adept at becoming whatever I need to be to win someone over. I've been everything to everyone, often simultaneously.

Coaching, therapy, and a strong personal/professional network have helped me embrace my challenges and become more constructive.

I understand that I feel shame when I make mistakes and that this feeling triggers a series of actions and thoughts that don't serve me. They zap my energy and bring me down. A solution-oriented mindset is fueled by curiosity, not shame.

So I seek a different perspective on my mistakes:

"Bad" news is just news if you don't judge it.

Mistakes are just lessons if you don't take them personally.

Shame keeps you static; curiosity enables movement and growth.
What would happen if joy was the goal, not perfection?

I was astounded by the swift response from folks—many of whom were also in leadership roles and shared my experience:

"Wow, does this resonate. Thank you for sharing!"

"I relate to this so hard. This is my M.O. as well. That shame can really set you back and get in your own way if you let it. Thank you for sharing."

"Oh my God this is so relatable! This speaks to me on so many levels."

"You've read my diary. Relatable 100%"

"Wow, did she just take these words and feelings right out of my head? This is me!!"

Another person shared my post and included this intro:

It's been a while since a LinkedIn post has stopped me dead in my tracks. This post from Devin did exactly this. The conversation I had with myself after reading this also surprised me so I figured I'd share in case others may be conflicted as well.

Here's how it went:

Goes and creeps her LinkedIn profile.

Oh wow, she is the CEO of Animalz. That was super brave of her to post such a vulnerable experience on LinkedIn given her position. I would never be able to do that!

Stares at screen a little while longer...

Wait, why wouldn't I? I admire her for doing it but tell myself I would never do that? Why?

I thought about this for a long while and realized it's because I, for some reason, equate being vulnerable as a weakness and something that may make me "less than" to my male peers and superiors. Yet, when I see a woman post something like this who I look up to and admire for what they've achieved professionally, I am wholeheartedly impressed.

Thank you, Devin, for sharing this so bravely. It's helped me realize I have some stuff to unpack on this front that is likely holding me back from living up to my full leadership potential. I appreciate you!

EMOTIONAL TARGETING: WIN HEARTS. BOOST SALES. OWN THE MARKET

Talia Wolf, *Founder and CEO, Getuplift*

Almost every single search includes emotion. The most common emotions that impact buying decisions are:

- **Self-image:** How people want to feel about themselves after finding a solution and converting.

- **Social image:** How people want others to feel about them after finding a solution and converting.

So when you're doing Conversion Rate Optimization (CRO), you're not just changing elements on a page, you're solving people's problems.

Successful CRO programs:

- answer critical business and customer questions

- run experiments that inform your whole marketing strategy

- break the silos between Marketing, Sales, and Product

Break the deadly hamster wheel of optimization by focusing on understanding your customers on a deeper level and solving their problems with your experiments.

What Happens If I Mess Up?

Consider an unhappy employee who rants to her coworkers and even her boss. If she truly didn't care, then she would simply leave the company. But she is *engaging*. People who don't care don't engage in passionate discussions.

This works in your favor because it actually takes a lot of effort just to get people to NOT like you. That's a lot of energy!

Which also means it's tough to fail. Most of the time, you're forgettable. You can do pretty embarrassing things and most folks won't even remember.

So it's all opportunity for you.

When it comes to your marketing strategy or plans it's kind of hard to fail.

Pretty much any marketing tactic you deploy will likely work a little or at the very least it won't make things materially worse. You'll just waste some time and money, but you have so little of that to begin with that it doesn't really matter.

And regardless, you'll get some valuable information from whatever you tried that will make your next attempt better. Logically, most of you know enough to at least not make things worse, because actually, it's hard to do that unless you're intentional about it.

Even if no one likes what you do, you'll learn from your mistakes more than doing nothing or trying to outperform someone else. You'll never know your limits if you don't test them.

> *No one dies if your content marketing sucks.*

Everything is developed by someone taking a lot of chances based on something that they think will work and every once in a while one of those things comes through as brilliance and originality. Don't be afraid to stumble along.

I dare you to be brave.

Conclusion: From Resonance to Results

Throughout this chapter, we've explored how to transform customer understanding into messaging and experiences that lead to action. The principles we've discussed aren't revolutionary—they're grounded in human psychology and marketing fundamentals—but applying them consistently will set you apart in a landscape dominated by commodity content.

Remember:

- no one cares about you (or your brand) until you make them care;
- resonance happens when you align with how people already see the world;
- your uniqueness is your advantage, but only when paired with audience relevance;
- authenticity can't be faked, but it can be cultivated;

- it takes courage to share original thoughts, but that's what creates true connection;
- your conviction, not your polish, is what makes content compelling.

In the following chapters, we'll move from resonance to results. We'll explore how to align your newly resonant messaging with the right channels and messengers, and how to create efficient content production systems that amplify your impact.

But before we move on, let's address a question you might be asking: "If resonance is so powerful, why does so much B2B content fall flat?"

The answer is simple: It's scarier. Creating content that genuinely resonates requires vulnerability. It means putting real thoughts and perspectives out there that might be challenged. It's more comfortable to hide behind generic "thought leadership" than to share authentic perspectives that might not resonate with everyone.

The path to resonance requires courage—the courage to stop talking about what you think people want to hear and start sharing what you actually believe. It demands the emotional intelligence to understand not just what your audience needs, but how they feel about those needs.

In other words, it requires you to recognize that marketing isn't about shouting louder than everyone else—it's about creating a signal that cuts through noise because it sounds different. Not because it's shocking or provocative, but because it's true in a way that makes people stop and think, "Finally, someone who gets it."

Notes

1 Stahl, S (2025) B2B content marketing benchmarks, budgets, and trends: Outlook for 2025 [Research] Contentmarketinginstitute.com, https://contentmarketinginstitute.com/b2b-research/b2b-content-marketing-trends-research (archived at https://perma.cc/CZT8-CLPU)

2 Content Marketing Institute (2023) 7 things B2B content marketers need in 2023 [New Research] https://contentmarketinginstitute.com/b2b-research/7-things-b2b-content-marketers-need-in-2023-new-research (archived at https://perma.cc/PML3-DBT5)

7

Aligning Channel, Message, and Messenger

Content marketing exists to serve business goals by solving customer pain points. That's it. Everything else—the channels, formats, distribution methods—these are just tools in service of that core mission.

The traditional customer journey framework fails because it gets three fundamental things wrong. It:

- assumes customers want to be led down a predetermined path (they don't);
- treats buying as a linear process with clear stages (it isn't);
- positions the brand as the conductor of the journey (we're not).

This matters because the way we visualize customer behavior shapes how we design our marketing. When we think in terms of linear journeys, we create rigid campaign structures designed to move people from Point A to Point B in a prescribed way. We obsess over "touchpoints" and "conversion paths" as if we're programming a GPS route to a destination.

This isn't just a metaphor—it's a mindset shift.

The companies that understand this are already changing how they market. Rather than mapping linear journeys, they're:

- building vibrant communities where their audience naturally gathers;
- creating content that encourages exploration rather than following a prescribed path;

FIGURE 7.1 Touchpoints

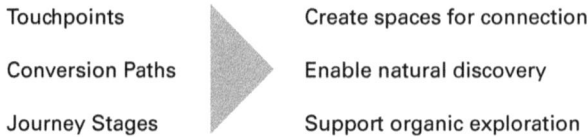

Touchpoints		Create spaces for connection
Conversion Paths		Enable natural discovery
Journey Stages		Support organic exploration

- enabling authentic connections between community members;
- letting customers help each other and share experiences.

This isn't just more effective—it's more sustainable. Instead of constantly pushing people down a predefined path, you're creating an environment that pulls people in and keeps them engaged through genuine value and connection.

> That's the power of community-driven growth—it creates lasting bonds that transcend typical business relationships and fuel ongoing expansion through authentic human connection.

Ashley Faus, senior marketing leader and author of *Human-Centered Marketing: How to Connect with Audiences in the Age of AI*, calls this the Content Playground:

> We need to think about the journey as a playground: People can go up, down, and sideways. They can go in any order. They can enter and exit as they please. And they can use content the "wrong" way. For example, pricing is traditionally considered a "bottom-of-funnel" conversation. However, if you are trying to secure budget for a new product or service, you need a sense of the price so that you can request enough money. It is no longer about rushing people to a purchase in as few touchpoints as possible; rather, it is about allowing them to choose their own path in a way that helps them reach their destination.

From Channels to Environments

When we shift from linear journey thinking to environment creation, we need a new framework for making decisions.

That framework is the harmony between channel, message, and messenger. Imagine these three elements as the legs of a tripod. When all three align perfectly, you create a stable foundation for effective marketing. If any leg is misaligned, the whole structure becomes unstable.

The most successful B2B companies don't try to be everywhere. They focus intensely on adding value on the channels where their audience already hangs out and engages naturally.

> Channel selection isn't about jumping on every trending platform or occupying the same spaces as your competitors. It's about understanding the natural habitat of the community.

Do they congregate in specific Slack communities? Are they active on certain subreddits? Do they attend certain events? Do they consume content in text, audio, or video format?

This isn't just about digital channels either. For some industries, physical spaces like conferences or local meetups might be more effective than any online platform. The key is to go where your audience already is, rather than trying to pull them to your preferred channels.

Find where your community hangs out. Ask to join by being altruistic. As I said in Chapter 3, hang out for a while, get to know folks and be authentic (i.e. brands, stop asking your internal influencers to post cringy stuff that is obviously not consistent with how they talk or what they contribute to the community).

B2B YOUTUBE STRATEGY

Finn McKenty, Marketing strategist, graphic designer and creator with 1.1 million followers

YouTube's algorithm can get you in front of 2.7 billion monthly active users, yet many companies still don't understand how to use it. They treat YouTube as a dumping ground for random videos. "Let's just throw it on YouTube" is *not* a strategy.

FIGURE 7.2 YouTube B2B

Two Ways to Use YouTube for B2B

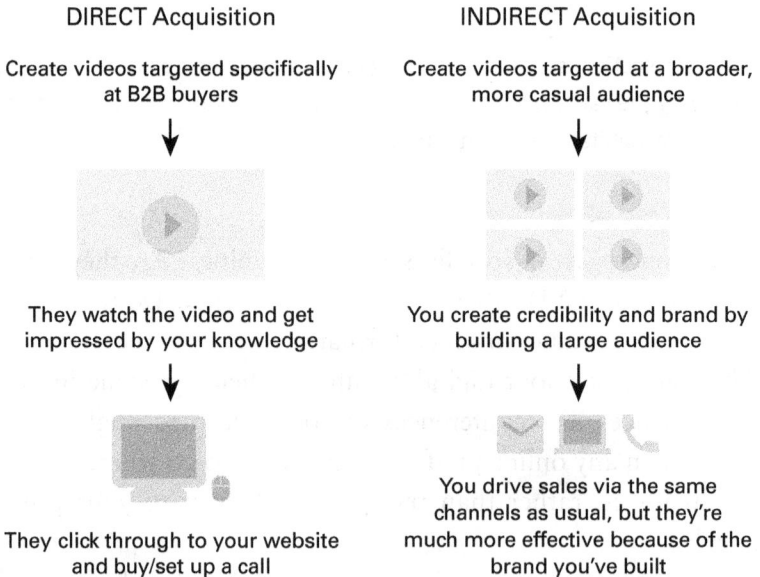

DIRECT Acquisition

Create videos targeted specifically at B2B buyers

↓

They watch the video and get impressed by your knowledge

↓

They click through to your website and buy/set up a call

INDIRECT Acquisition

Create videos targeted at a broader, more casual audience

↓

You create credibility and brand by building a large audience

↓

You drive sales via the same channels as usual, but they're much more effective because of the brand you've built

Finn McKenty

There are two ways that B2B companies can use YouTube to grow:

DIRECT ACQUISITION

Goal: *Get business directly from YouTube.*

Make videos for your ICP, include a CTA, and hope that they click through and buy from you. Example: Creating a video called "How to integrate WooCommerce with Memberium memberships."

In this scenario, you won't get a lot of views, but the people who *do* click will be very high-intent. Companies can achieve defensible ROI if they can sell 2 percent of them a $10k implementation package.

INDIRECT ACQUISITION

Goal: *Use YouTube to make your other acquisition channels more effective (essentially, this is brand marketing).*

Build a big audience on the larger topic of e-commerce. Do breakdowns of well-known e-commerce brands (Skims, Ridge, Native, etc.) that get 50–100k views and you become an authority in the space.

Then when you meet someone at a conference, DM them on LinkedIn, and they already know who you are and they're 10x more likely to do business with you.

In general, I think indirect acquisition has the most upside. It takes more lateral thinking than just grinding out SEO videos, but I think the long-term potential is way, way higher.

From Messages to Meaning

The more precisely you can speak to the specific needs, challenges, and aspirations of your community using language they are familiar with to describe their *actual* situation—not your perception of their situation—the more your message will resonate.

Each channel "behaves" differently depending on the community and, to a small degree, the platform norms themselves. The latter is less important, because most communities adapt the channel to their desires and ultimately end up spreading out into ad hoc subgroups elsewhere. That said, there are obvious norms, which you don't need me to tell you and which will evolve over time anyway, but I promised I would, so at the very least I'll keep it short:

- **LinkedIn:** Work stuff. Networking, prospecting, audience building, selling.
- **Slack:** Creating community around shared interests. Free Slack groups created by a small group of people in, say, B2B marketing (I'm in two). Paid Slack groups that are part of a creator offering or community platform like Pavilion.

- **YouTube:** Entertainment, mostly. Learning falls under that category as well, because those seeking out education are usually doing so on behalf of their own personal interests and hobbies.

- **Newsletters:** Typically for enthusiasts—folks who want to get into the weeds on a topic for deeper learning for personal or professional reasons. Also, fans of a particular person who want more content and a personal experience with them. The unifying factor is that both groups are independently motivated to subscribe, even if it's "for work."

- **Conferences:** Sales, relationship development, brand awareness, and credibility or product launch hype and other types of marketing objectives. For solopreneurs, conferences are typically where they fill up their funnel and get new clients, grow their audience and credibility, sell their ideas or services. (Notice I didn't include learning? That's just the smoke and mirrors to get people to come.)

Creating meaning isn't just about what you say, it's about how you say it in each environment. Make sure you're starting conversations that are organic to the environment you're engaging in. The same core information might be framed very differently in different places.

For instance, when discussing a new approach to data security:

- on LinkedIn, you might frame it as a career advancement opportunity;

- in a technical Slack community, you'd focus on implementation details;

- in your email newsletter, you could provide a comprehensive analysis;

- at a conference, you'd emphasize the strategic implications.

From Messenger to Community

Who delivers your message matters as much as the message itself.

The right messenger brings credibility and connection that brand channels simply can't accomplish on their own. These folks speak the language of your community and know their sub-level challenges. In most cases, they are existing members of the community who elevated themselves by being prolific and offering value to their peers.

> When you are choosing a messenger, it's best to start with folks who already have credibility in the community.

However, credibility does not necessarily mean "fame" i.e. lots of followers. Some of the most effective messengers hate giving talks and making YouTube videos—and you don't need them to either. These messenger types built their credibility through their knowledge, ideas, and desire to help. They are unique in a way that adds net new value to the community just by being who they are. Your only job with these messengers is to support what they are already doing and identify new containers for them to fill that are designed around *them*, because they are a proxy for either all or a segment of your community.

REAL-WORLD EXAMPLE
Influence Versus Fame

The current prevailing definition of an "influencer" is someone who has a lot of followers on one or more social platforms and/or a high volume of subscribers, listeners, and other means of directly opting in to them. To me that definition is as accurate as measuring total website traffic. What's more important is the depth and frequency at which they engage with you, quote things that you say, and recommend you to others.

It's hard not to fall into the fame trap, because seeing those simple numbers get bigger and bigger does feel good! Even knowing this, I still obsessed over listener and subscriber numbers when I launched *Don't Say Content*, a podcast I co-created with my friend and fellow marketer, Margaret Kelsey. We agreed from the beginning that our intended audience were marketing leaders (Directors, VPs, C-suite), which we knew would drastically reduce potential listener volume. Yet I still found myself chasing listener volume and brainstorming campaigns that would get us more newsletter subscribers. Meanwhile, we were racking up 5-star reviews, being listed in top marketing podcast roundups and receiving countless personal messages from our ICP praising the show, noting the positive impact it had on them.

What I realized later was that it was our own influence that helped grow the show. We were the influencers that gave the show credibility and appeal, even though our personal follower counts were not that high. It didn't matter because the folks who did follow us were mostly the marketing leaders we were speaking to in our show.

There are several common, effective messenger types, some of whom are already in your closest orbit:

- Internal subject matter experts?
- Current customers?
- Industry thought leaders?
- Community moderators?
- Specific executives within your organization?

The challenge here is allowing your messengers to speak in their unique voice while still maintaining the message. You don't want them to sound like brand robots as that lack of authenticity is a surefire way for your message to misfire. My friend, creative director and content strategist Arestia Rosenberg, is dynamite at getting this to align. She works with agencies, startups, and brands to help them hone their stories and give them not just language they can use, but guidelines that get all their employees speaking the same language (I know this because I've done this with her for a couple of clients myself!).

One recent startup she worked with needed an overhaul as their company was pivoting from a B2C to a B2B brand. All the language and messaging their current employees were using wasn't going to cut it anymore, and on top of that, they were growing like crazy and hiring many more new employees. She needed to get everyone aligned in speaking the same language—and fast.

She first had conversations with several employees at every level. Then she worked to create voice guidelines that she first ran by the C-suite before rolling them out to the rest of the company. Those guidelines included general boilerplate copy they should use/keep in mind like the mission, tagline, and positioning, but also described the voice, persona, and gave five words as brand pillars. With each word, she described why they should write/sound this way when talking about the company, gave some dos and don'ts, and some specific examples for what that might sound like in things like an email, a slack group, or even with a direct conversation with a client. She also provided a glossary of terminology and a checklist they should review every time they communicated.

All of this was delivered in an onboarding meeting where people could ask questions and at the end everyone was encouraged to print out the slide deck filled with all this gold to keep with them and review. The deck wasn't meant to be prescriptive but to guide them in their communication, and help them if they were ever doubtful in what and how they were communicating. She also presented this "voice guidelines workshop" during all the new employees' onboarding.

Within weeks, everyone was speaking the same language—in their own way.

The point is, you want to equip your people with a way to communicate clearly and consistently, without stripping away what makes them sound like them. Provide them with a shared language, not a script, because when everyone knows the story, they'll be able to tell it in a way that will carry your message further.

Finding Your Sweet Spot

When you align all three elements—channel, message, and messenger—you'll create marketing that feels natural, valuable, and perfectly suited to your audience's preferences. To find your sweet spot, use this matrix to evaluate potential marketing initiatives

This matrix helps explain why so many B2B marketing efforts fail despite huge investments. A company might create great content (high message alignment) and have the perfect messenger, but if they're distributing it on a channel their audience doesn't use (low channel alignment), they'll see poor results.

THREE SHIFTS IN CONTENT ENGAGEMENT

Fajr Muhammad, *VP of Content Strategy and Growth at iPullRank*

With AI Overviews, zero-click, and AI summaries, getting someone to click through is a win but it's also just the beginning. We can no longer assume a click = deep engagement. Now it's about depth over vanity.

ENGAGEMENT METRICS ARE CHANGING
It's not about getting seen. It's about being remembered.

Content engagement is no longer linear and things like pageviews, likes, and clicks are not enough to indicate true interest. Depth of engagement—time spent, scroll depth, saves, duration, return visits, subscribes—are the new priority metrics to watch.

CONTENT NEEDS TO BE WORTHY TO STOP THE SCROLL
Scroll-stopping content starts before it's even created.

Breaking through to your audience means understanding them on a deeper level. What do they want to see, where do they want to see it, and how do they want to see it? Stopping the scroll means being worthy of your audience's attention.

POST-CLICK BEHAVIOR IS MORE VALUABLE
Making the most of a visit is crucial.

Instead of going for the big swing, try micro-conversions or "second steps" to get valuable information from the visitors. Incentives and FOMO are strong drivers. Email capture and tracking pixels allow for remarketing and retargeting.

The benefit of an orbit-type approach is that it helps brands stand out from competition (even if competition is taking the same approach—I'll explain more in this chapter). You need people to develop ideas, not necessarily to create them. Your customers are a treasure trove of ideas. Even fragments of ideas can come from anywhere. To make use of them, you have to keep an open mind. Relating disparate things together is hard, not natural for everyone, but if you're focused on solving a problem or developing an idea, they will come to you more naturally because it's top of mind. What you focus on becomes your life.

DEVIN'S CLEVER ALIGNMENT STRATEGY

This is mostly a template for your boss. It's a sort of copy-and-paste you can adapt to explain your approach if need be. Something translatable, digestible, and also flexible enough that you can execute (and hide) any number of activities within it.

STEP 1: IDENTIFY HIGHEST-IMPACT OPPORTUNITIES

These high-alignment opportunities are where you should focus your initial efforts.

Look for the most overlap between:

- channel(s) where your audience is actively engaged
- message you're uniquely qualified to deliver
- messenger with natural credibility in that space

STEP 2: DESIGN EXPERIMENTS

Rather than launching a massive campaign across all channels right away, this framework begins with rapid experiments in your highest-alignment areas that you can test and refine.

For each experiment, choose your components:

- channel
- message you're testing
- messenger who will deliver it
- metrics that will indicate it's working

STEP 3: MEASURE ALIGNMENT, NOT JUST OUTCOMES

When evaluating your experiments, look beyond simple conversion metrics to measure alignment itself:

- channel alignment: engagement rate, time spent, return visits
- message alignment: relevance feedback, comment sentiment, sharing behavior
- messenger alignment: credibility ratings, relationship building, follower growth

STEP 4: EXPAND

Once you've identified high-alignment combinations, systematically expand your presence while maintaining alignment. This might mean:

- deepening your presence in successful channels before adding new ones

- expanding your message to address related topics
- developing additional messengers who can maintain authentic connections

Measuring Success in a Nonlinear World

It's time to meet the elephant in the room. His name is Mili, and he has a question:

If we're creating environments rather than funnels, how do we track success?

FAIR, Mili.

The answer, obviously, isn't to abandon measurement—you need to play along and most likely you have a metric assigned to you already. But you also want to see if what you're doing is working, so let's address both.

Working the Stakeholders

The simplest way to connect marketing activities that can't be measured in software to your assigned metric is to be Cinderella's stepsister and find a way to make that big, ugly foot fit into the glass slipper. You're a storyteller, so tell a story! Convince them that everything really is a nail. To do this well, you do need to get comfy with *some* data analysis, but I learned fractions with donuts, so you'll be fine.

Another option is to put activities that can't be measured in software into an "experiments" category or an appendix slide and essentially hide them to avoid attention. This is helpful if you're doing something that's showing signals, but your CFO is reading it and you don't want to deal with their, er, lack of range. But this can work for your CEO and investors, too. The business folks who want short, simple answers and don't get marketing anyway.

This next one is similar and tends to work best on the CEO. Drag them into the weeds with *lots* of data and details to make them bored and impatient so they want you to go away. Just don't use it on your CFO, CTO, or if you're working with an early-stage CEO. Your CFO, CTO, or even an investor or board member is more likely to dissect this just for fun, so it's not worth the squeeze and honestly, they'll likely "win," which would make things worse.

And early-stage founders, let's just say the chaotic acid trip of a conversation you're inviting is like bidding in one of those storage space auctions and you win the one that contains something different every time you open it.

How to Evaluate What's Working

Think of this section like a brainstorm. What I'm sharing are ideas and options you can consider. Adapt, combine, play, just don't feel confined by this list.

The truth is, you know the resonant hum when you see it, but since businesses don't operate on vibrations, experiment with the options that make sense to you and see what resonates with stakeholders.

- **Community engagement**
  - active participation rates
  - conversation depth (not just volume)
  - peer-to-peer connections formed
  - user-generated content volume
  - return frequency and duration
- **Influence**
  - message adoption and language use
  - third-party citations and references
  - share of voice in industry conversations
  - expert status indicators (speaking invitations, etc.)
  - decision influence in buying committees

- **Relationship strength**
  - multi-person engagement from target accounts
  - depth of interaction across content types
  - willingness to provide feedback
  - brand advocacy behaviors
  - sales conversation quality (not just quantity)

Conclusion: From Funnels to Ecosystems

The traditional marketing funnel is dead. Actually, it was never alive to begin with—just a mental model we created to make sense of the messy reality of how people make decisions. That model served us for a while, but now it's hindering more than it's helping.

What I've shared in this chapter—the three-way alignment of channel, message, and messenger—represents a fundamental shift in how we approach B2B marketing. Instead of creating rigid funnels and trying to force prospects through them, we're building rich ecosystems where our audience naturally wants to participate.

This approach acknowledges the reality of how B2B decisions actually happen: through conversations, recommendations, random discoveries, and multiple cycles of evaluation. Decision-making isn't linear—it's organic, social, and often unpredictable. Our marketing should reflect that reality.

The magic happens when all three elements come together:

- **Channels** that respect where your audience already spends time
- **Messages** that align with their existing mindset in each context
- **Messengers** who bring natural credibility and authenticity

This alignment creates marketing that doesn't feel like marketing at all. It feels like valuable information from trusted sources in places where people are already spending time. And that's precisely why it works.

I've seen the power of this alignment in my own work—from The Springpad Show's community-building effect to the surprising impact of authentic voices at Animalz. I've witnessed it in companies like Gong, who leveraged their unique data access, and in solopreneurs creating niche communities around shared interests.

The best part? This approach is more efficient, not less. When you focus on high-alignment opportunities rather than trying to be everywhere at once, you create deeper connections with less effort. You stop wasting resources on channels where your message won't resonate or with messengers who don't carry natural credibility.

This doesn't mean abandoning measurement—it means measuring what actually matters. Instead of obsessing over touchpoints and conversion paths, focus on community engagement, influence indicators, and relationship strength. These metrics might not fit neatly into your analytics dashboard, but they reflect the real drivers of business growth.

As you move forward, remember that finding your alignment sweet spot is an ongoing process, not a one-time exercise. Your audience's preferences will evolve. New channels will emerge. Different messengers will resonate at different times. The key is building a system that can adapt to these changes while maintaining the core alignment principle.

In the next chapter, we'll explore how to design an efficient content marketing plan that leverages media-first thinking and AI to bring this aligned approach to life at scale. We'll show how starting with rich media assets and using AI as a multiplication tool lets you maintain authentic presence across multiple touchpoints without exhausting your team or budget.

The companies that master this alignment gain a sustainable advantage that goes beyond any single campaign or tactic. They build environments their audience wants to be part of, share messages that genuinely resonate, and empower messengers their audience actually trusts.

That's not just good marketing—it's good business.

8

Designing an Efficient Content Marketing Plan Using Media and AI

If you think about it, you and me and everyone we know, we're all asking the same question over and over. It appears in different forms, but the fundamental question we keep asking as if it's a lottery ticket that maybe this time will finally have a winning answer, it's always the same: *What should I do?* And then there's the popular follow up: *How do I do it?*

The exact scenario the question applies to—and its gravity—varies greatly, of course. How do I advance in my marketing career? Where do I start on this campaign I pitched but don't really know how to execute? What's the best way to boil an egg? How do I write the perfect blog post (and also can you tell me what the criteria for perfect are)? What are the eight best ways to achieve everything in the world: the perfect body, a partner, my career, total and consistent bliss forever into infinity!

It's good to ask questions and get advice from people you trust, particularly for those big life questions. But when it comes to creative work, how productive is it to ask for a roadmap?

Dear Abby, what specific steps (in order of execution) do I need to produce this exact thing I saw someone else do, because damn it's hard to come up with my own ideas...

Not that a little creative copying is a bad idea. Imitating someone you admire is a great way to develop skills, unlock inspiration, and discover your own unique style. In my mid-twenties, I read a lot of Tom Robbins, Chuck Palahniuk, and Hunter S. Thompson, and their influence is all over my writing from that time. Everything I wrote for two years reeked of wannabe, and I thought it was delicious, like the rum and pineapple cocktail I began drinking because it was Thompson's drink of choice in *The Rum Diary*.

But when you're asking the "what should I do" questions in creative pursuits, you bypass the winding road that leads to ideas that have never been had before.

Elements of Strategy

The purpose of content marketing as a strategy is to grow businesses by solving customer pain points.

That's it. Everything else—the channels, formats, distribution methods—these are tools in service of that core mission. They are also not the only tools you can use in service of achieving your target outcomes. On a similar note, because you're creating a content marketing strategy doesn't mean you have to use all the content marketing tools available to you.

In fact, the most effective strategies center on a few objectives to achieve your desired outcomes rather than trying to cover all possible ground, a concept I learned in Richard Rumelt's book *Good Strategy, Bad Strategy*. Instead, it's about concentrating your resources on a few realistic goals.

Here's a good example of what that looks like in practice:

CREATING EXPONENTIAL IMPACT AT SIGMA
Emily Anne Epstein, *Director of Content at Sigma*

Content isn't here to fill space—it's how we grow. And real growth means creating momentum that doesn't stop at pageviews.

When I joined Sigma, my first focus was SEO content. Traffic was strong. Performance? Not so much. People were reading, but they weren't doing anything afterward. The calls-to-action didn't match the user journey—and we were losing people who might've wanted more.

It's a familiar challenge in B2B. You invest in quality content. You bring in organic traffic. But the journey stops short. A static "View Demo" button at the top and a generic CTA at the bottom aren't going to convert someone who's still figuring out their problem—let alone whether you're the right solution.

The issue wasn't with the content itself. It was with the experience surrounding it. We were giving every reader the same next step, regardless of why they showed up or what they needed. That's how you lose attention: by not respecting the intent behind it.

We needed a better system—something flexible, something scalable. Updating CTAs manually wasn't going to cut it. I wanted a way to serve dynamic, relevant CTAs that met people where they were *and* gave our team the control to iterate fast.

That's when we started thinking about our content like ad inventory.

We spent budget on external ads all the time. But what about our own site—the place where visitors already know us, already care enough to click? Why not use that space more deliberately?

I brought the idea to Pete Hawkes, our Head of Web, and he built it: a plugin that lets us manage and serve CTAs like an internal ad network. Now, every blog post has four dynamic placements. We can test messages, adjust targeting, and change every CTA across the site from a single interface.

And the payoff? Clear and fast:

- time on site went up 118 percent
- pages per session grew by 13 percent
- influenced pipeline increased, directly tied to these changes

Before, the average visit lasted 90 seconds and hit 1.2 pages. After the update, we saw three-minute sessions and 1.35 pages per visit. Not a massive jump on paper, but when you're talking thousands of visits per month, those extra seconds and clicks translate into meaningful engagement.

Best of all, this wasn't just a win for content. It helped our sales team. It gave demand gen more levers to pull. It surfaced product messaging in high-value places. When content systems work like this—cross-functionally, strategically—that's when the real impact happens.

Emily's approach was strategic on several dimensions:

- could logically be executed
- served multiple business goals
- could be executed and maintained with existing resources
- produced exponential impact
- grounded in facts, not best practices

She demonstrated the positive outcomes companies see when they identify their leverage points and focus intensely on those areas, see the ripple effects amplify their success. They aren't following playbooks, they're writing them.

Once you discover something that works, then you can leverage AI to scale your operations or extract more value from what you're already doing.

Using AI: Practical and Systematic Application

When it comes to incorporating AI into your content marketing engine there are two applications that I believe cover most use-cases relevant to content marketers. Since the technology is still evolving at a rapid pace and there are near-infinite ways you can use AI to benefit your content marketing programs, I'm going to focus on how to approach incorporating AI. Ultimately, what you do will depend greatly on your own investment, the tools you have control over at your company, what you can use without approval, and what you can convince your company to adopt.

As it relates to adoption, I recommend using the advice and tactics in Chapters 9 and 11 to help you strategize around that.

Practical: AI as a Tool

Think: prompts, transcriptions, research, data analysis, competitor analysis, helping you brainstorm, content atomization, etc. (If you're looking for more help with this, I recommend picking up Pam Didner's books.)

Systematic: Powered by AI

Automate aspects of your work that don't see strategic benefit from human execution. It can also help in areas where you lack skillsets or simply don't enjoy the work. NOTE: You'll likely need a tech person to help you create but it's a defensible use of their time and you can quantify that to higher-ups if needed to get approval. My best advice here is to think of the exact automations, reports, functionality, etc., you've always wanted—the stuff that seems impossible—and start there.

Not sure what to ask for? I asked ChatGPT how it could support me on the book and it gave me a list of suggestions like looking for repeats of ideas or stories, or evaluating chapters as a specific persona to spot gaps.

THERE'S NO SUCH THING AS "SEO CONTENT"

Mike King, *Founder of SEO, Content Strategy, and Generative AI at iPullRank.*

Modern content strategy isn't about hacking an algorithm. It's about meeting audience expectations, delivering high-quality experiences, and ensuring content is both useful and accessible. When content aligns with audience personas, buyer personas, and search engine expectations, it doesn't just rank—it converts and then it keeps ranking.

The idea of "SEO content" is outdated because there's no such thing as content that is only for search engines. Google's algorithms have evolved beyond simple keyword matching and word count assessments. Instead, they focus on semantic meaning, contextual relevance, and user engagement.

The term "SEO content" itself suggests that content exists in two categories: One for search engines and another for actual people. That thinking is outdated.

Search engines prioritize content that is well-structured, useful, and aligned with audience needs, and they can verify this by evaluating how users interact with your content when it appears in the search engine results page (SERP).

SEO isn't about gaming algorithms. It's about creating content where the expectations of audience personas, buyer personas, and search engines intersect.

Getting Started: Outlining Your Plan

Here's a pretty simple approach to creating your content marketing plan that will help you make important decisions around what to include and exclude, how to get buy-in and measure success.

For the tactics within your plan, since you already know what I recommend, I'm including knowledge and ideas from some of the smartest marketers to give you more options and perspectives than I can on my own. More options = more leverage.

Start with Business Goals

Every content strategy needs to tie back to concrete business objectives regardless of how we as marketers feel about the legitimacy of some of those connections. Doing so not only allows us to continue doing our jobs but let's face it: Creatives need constraints. We need to know the endpoint we're trying to get to in order to make content that has impact on the business. We'll talk more about communicating non-numerical impact to stakeholders in the next chapter. For now, make sure you create a plan that not only addresses your stated goal, but also enables you to speak to unspoken priorities among stakeholders:

- revenue targets
- customer acquisition goals
- market positioning goals
- brand awareness metrics

Identify Resources and Constraints

Be realistic about what you can achieve with your resources:

- budget limitations
- team capacity
- marketing direct reports and peers
- other departments
- internal influencers (important to be in reality about how much they can/will contribute)
- community support, champions
- technical capabilities and tools
- time constraints

Based on your goals and constraints, select the spaces and tactics that will return the greatest impact:

- channels
- messengers and messages
- content types
- campaigns

Hypothesize Results and Outcomes

Important for measuring any experiments, track success so you can report on it every week and show trends in positive motion. Crucial to this part of your plan is outlining what could go wrong. You will gain more trust faster by bringing potential risks out in the open from the beginning than you will by claiming you anticipated them (without telling anyone) after they happen. This is your opportunity to leverage or lose:

- What outcomes are you trying to achieve and by when?
- Are there variables in possible results? If so, what do you estimate those are?
- What are the blockers to launching? How do you plan on overcoming them?
- What are the risks of this plan? How will you mitigate those risks?
- Is there a better version of this plan that is outside your budget that stakeholders should consider?
- What will you do next if your plan works?

Execute

Make that project plan. Set milestones and break them down into key results with due dates and hold your team to them. This isn't just about making sure the project gets done. It's about creating finite circumstances you can learn from and report on later when evaluating what worked and what needs improvement.

Evangelize your plan internally: Create a one-pager for an internal campaign summarizing strategy, objectives, experiments, high-level risks, etc. It's a way of inviting people into marketing without leaving a lot of space for input.

Keep the company updated along the way: Wanna know how to keep leadership off your back? Proactively share things that didn't go to plan, reflect on them, ask for input, and share your hypothesis for improvement. Same goes for wins. Leaders don't like being surprised, even when the news is good, so small updates more consistently will always win over a crescendo report at the end of the month or quarter.

Scale what works: The obvious final step! This will be easier to get buy-in for if you execute following the communication tactics above.

REAL-WORLD EXAMPLE
State of the Interactive Product Demo

Navattic is a software platform that helps sales and marketing teams create interactive product demos. *The State of the Interactive Product Demo* is an annual report the company publishes for their customers and prospects who want up-to-date information about demo best practices. They noticed that the ways their customers use demos are constantly changing, so they publish it annually to ensure they're providing the most current information to their community.

"The objective was to educate customers and prospects who were looking for best practices before they started creating demos. We promote the report to create buzz around interactive demos and answer common prospect objections," Natalie Marcotullio, Head of Growth and Product Marketing, explains.

She measured ROI on 3 dimensions:

- traffic to the landing page as well as lift in traffic to other pages from the report landing page;

- lead volume: how many folks convert to customers from that segment;

- content repurposing: using it as the basis for customer interview series, podcasts, webinars, and other blog posts throughout the year.

In 2024, it was their highest-trafficked page (besides the homepage) and one of their highest-converting landing pages resulting in approximately 200 pre-launch early access signups, two times more visitors than the previous year's report and 19 new customer stories created from the report then repurposed into YouTube videos, blogs, and short-form social posts.

Why this worked: They kept it simple. They identified something their customers felt was crucial to doing their job well, created a resource with the intent to *help* their customers first, and built a strategy around it that served both short-term KPIs (traffic and signups) and contributed to other growth efforts she had planned for the year.

FRAMEWORK FOR MAXIMIZING CONTENT
Kym Meyer, SVP of Media Strategy

In a world where organic reach is declining and paid media costs are increasing, getting maximum mileage from every piece of content isn't just efficient—it's essential for sustainable marketing. This approach allows you to maintain consistent messaging while adapting to each channel's unique requirements and audience expectations with the assistance of AI tools.

1. START WITH RICH MEDIA

Begin with video or audio content (interviews, discussions, presentations). This becomes your "source material" for all other content formats. Example: Record a one-hour conversation with your CEO or subject matter expert.

2. MAP CONTENT TO CUSTOMER JOURNEY

Before atomizing your content, identify how it maps to different stages of the customer journey:

- **Awareness stage:** Educational content that addresses broad industry challenges.
- **Pain point stage:** Content that dives deeper into specific problems your solution addresses.
- **Consideration stage:** More product-focused content that demonstrates your solution.

This mapping ensures your content serves specific purposes across the funnel and helps you identify which channels are most appropriate for distribution.

3. CREATE ADAPTABLE CONTENT ACROSS MULTIPLE FORMATS

Content should be adaptable for each channel you use while maintaining consistent core messaging, with the same core material formatted as:

- **Written:** narratives, lists, guides.
- **Video:** executive interviews, testimonials, how-to demonstrations.
- **Designed:** newsletters, listicles, infographics.

This adaptability allows you to create channel-specific versions:

- **LinkedIn newsletter**
  - transform key insights into newsletter format
  - benefits: reaches engaged in-platform audience + sends to subscribers' inboxes
  - creates discoverable, indexed pages on LinkedIn and Google Search
  - generates comments and engagement beyond your database

- **Company blog/resource pages**
  - edit and expand the content for your website
  - optimize for SEO to capture search traffic
  - include more comprehensive information than social versions
- **LinkedIn page and executive posts**
  - create condensed versions of key points
  - use as standalone posts or to promote the newsletter/blog content
  - posts from actual people (executives, customers, partners) outperform company page posts in engagement and traffic
- **Email nurtures**
  - incorporate content into your email nurture sequences
  - customize based on audience segments and buyer journey stages
  - test reformatting and different content layouts to increase open rates

4. STRATEGIC PAID AMPLIFICATION

Use paid promotion to boost organic content that shows strong engagement while SEO content builds quality scores. Particularly effective in the first 90 days of content publication. Options include:

- making content the landing page for relevant campaigns
- adding as a sitelink to existing programs
- boosting social posts that perform well organically
- using LinkedIn's "creator promoted" ad unit for individual posts

5. LEVERAGE INTERNAL EXPERTS AND EXTERNAL VOICES

Focus on promoting people over company pages:

- executive content drives more engagement than brand pages alone
- coach executives on reach and engagement growth
- tap into experts across the organization for diverse content

Extend reach through partnerships:

- customer spotlights and case studies
- industry influencer collaborations
- participation in podcasts, panels, and other speaking engagements

6. MEASURE AND OPTIMIZE

Track both engagement metrics and revenue impact:

- social engagement: likes, comments, views

- traffic: site visits, resource page views

- revenue impact: form field for "how did you hear about us?"

Develop dashboards for goal tracking:

- real-time metrics for resource pages

- topic and page performance tracking

- review weekly by platform, region, audience, and messaging themes

CONSIDERATIONS

You lose some personalization capabilities when using platform-specific formats like LinkedIn templates:

- building audience on platforms means starting lists from scratch (though you can promote to existing audiences);

- platform metrics may not contribute directly to MQL scoring or lead progression like owned channels do;

- video content is particularly "sticky" in social feeds but requires additional production resources.

Avoid These Pitfalls, If You Can

Obsessing over Small Details

For whose benefit are you grammar-policing? Do your customers care about the types of edits you're making? Is it necessary for them to understand the meaning and information you are trying to communicate?

Focusing Too Much on Activity, Not Impact

While activity metrics are an important part of understanding the impact of your work (which I will go into more in the next chapter), make sure you're not falling into a popularity trap. It is indeed possible to create a lot of buzz that does not translate into adequate business impact, and the constraint of ROI only challenges you to think more creatively. Don't resist it. While many marketing activities lack 1:1 bottom line impact, it's your job to develop a resonant story for your stakeholders that ties the two together. Practice makes improvement. Experimentation makes progress.

USING PAID MEDIA TO TEST BRAND MESSAGING AND BUILD AN AUDIENCE
Kristin Young

Promoting your videos and serving targeted ads on the channels your audience already follow on YouTube is a good approach for building your audience. You can then leverage that audience in your marketing funnel in a couple of ways.

HONE YOUR AUDIENCE, MAXIMIZE YOUR BUDGET
People who engage with your videos can be used as a Google Ads audience to run retargeting campaigns against. This approach helps you narrow the budget based on the criteria of people you're looking to reach on the platform, which is particularly useful for companies that are early in their messaging exploration.

TEST MULTIPLE MESSAGES
A strategy that works well within Google Ads on YouTube is targeting specific channels that people are already following. You can use tools like SparkToro, which are good at analyzing YouTube channels by specifying, "For people who visit this website or people who follow these people, here are some YouTube channels that they're following." Then you can run ads against that cohort.

Here's an example: Run display or text ads with your message against xyz channels and/or people who watch those channels to determine which value prop appeals to your community. For this, I suggest running very basic campaigns that only look at engagement as a means of building the case for down-funnel tactics (i.e. Message 2 resonates the most, so this is our Stage 1). Though this only works if you have enough budget to run the test at the appropriate size and reach.

You cannot effectively test multiple messages with a small budget.

I recommend companies with small budgets pick one message and go down the rabbit hole with it from there. It's a strategic framework for cost-efficiently testing messaging. Use paid search to test one message, edit and make it work and then build your campaigns on that message. To be considered a "winner," it has to meet the success metrics you defined at each stage.

Once you build your framework and understand your conversion rates all the way down the funnel, you can use that as a baseline for every new message or channel that you want to test. This approach works especially well for companies at 0–1 who need quick wins and only have a limited budget.

Neglecting the Future

Content marketing is both a short- and long-term game. The most effective content strategies account for the future while serving short- and medium-term objectives. While capitalizing on one-off opportunities that return outsized results will likely be consistent players, making them the objects of your strategy is often inefficient and less effective long-term:

- build systems that are sustainable and scale
- build relationships with execs and across departments
- make repeatable things that become objects on a shelf
- build relationships with influencers

Not Experimenting

The landscape changes too quickly to stick with one approach:

- regular testing of new formats and channels
- controlled experiments with messaging and positioning
- data-driven iteration on what works
- willingness to fail and learn

Conclusion: Making Efficiency Your Competitive Advantage

The most effective B2B marketers don't just create content—they build systems that generate exponential impact from limited resources.

By starting with rich media, strategically atomizing across channels, and selectively leveraging AI, they create sustainable frameworks that grow and evolve with their organization.

Throughout this chapter, we've explored practical approaches to designing efficient content plans that deliver real business results:

- **Start with strategy, not tactics.** When you begin with clear business objectives and understand your unique advantages and constraints, you naturally focus on the highest-impact activities rather than trying to do everything.

- **Create once, distribute strategically.** By starting with rich media and thoughtfully adapting to each channel's requirements, you maximize the value of every piece of content you create while maintaining consistent messaging.

- **Use AI as a multiplier, not a replacement.** AI offers tremendous efficiency gains when applied thoughtfully—whether streamlining research, supporting content atomization, or enabling personalization at scale.

- **Build systems, not campaigns.** Rather than one-off initiatives, focus on creating repeatable frameworks that deliver compounding returns over time and can evolve with changing market conditions.

- **Test, learn, and adapt.** The most successful content systems include deliberate experimentation and continuous improvement based on real-world results.

Remember, the best strategy is one you can actually execute. Start with the principles we've covered but adapt them to your reality. Focus on building systems that can grow and evolve with your organization.

Most importantly, keep your eye on the fundamental truth: Content marketing exists to serve business goals by solving customer pain points. When you maintain this focus while building efficient, scalable systems, you transform content from a resource-intensive obligation into a genuine competitive advantage.

9

Measuring and Reporting on Content Marketing Strategy

The foundation of effective content marketing strategy is that measurement should serve strategy, not define it.

How do you measure if this is working?

That wasn't my CEO asking me about a marketing strategy I proposed or campaign I planned to run. That was a reporter asking a policeman about a new initiative he'd launched to keep illegal scooters off the streets in his city. Folks had been stealing them then committing crimes and using stolen bikes made it hard for the police to track—and catch—the robbers.

The policeman's response went something like: *Well, if at the end of tonight we don't see a shooting and no one gets hurt from the community and none of our cops get hurt, we will take that as a win.*

My mouth dropped in disbelief and I was stunned into frustrated silence, because I had just learned that police officers, who are responsible for people's lives, were being held to looser attribution standards than B2B content marketers.

Ok, ok, a little dramatic, but the thing I couldn't stop thinking about was that this police officer proudly stated his attribution model and was praised for it. Like, the reporter congratulated him and so did the news anchors. It was even written in the paper and everyone was fine with his answer.

Meanwhile, I was defending a successful content marketing program to my CEO yet again with better success metrics than the guy whose job it is to report on keeping people alive!

There is a useful lesson here, which is that performance reporting is often more about public relations than it is about communicating what really happened, so a lot of what I share in this chapter will focus on the researching, experimenting, and campaigning pieces of reporting, as those tend to be the most useful.

My ultimate goal with this chapter is to convince you to get really good at reporting to the point where you enjoy doing it and see it as an opportunity to create leverage for yourself. Ultimately, practice is what will teach you the most, which means you are going fall on your face a bit along the way. You'll defend performance metrics that you'll later realize aren't important or do math wrong and stuff like that. It's part of the process, so learn from it then let yourself off the hook. Because here's the thing no one tells you: *All along the way, people higher up the corporate hierarchy, who should definitely know better, read your report and didn't even notice.*

Before I dive in, though, I want to make sure we're operating from the same belief:

KEY POINT

Marketers have the **ideal brains and skillsets** to deeply analyze quantitative and qualitative data and make meaning out of it that helps businesses grow and benefits their personal career agenda.

The only reason you, yes *you*, haven't been able to do that yet is because you believe something about yourself that isn't true. Wanna know how I know?

I had zero special skills or training that would make me even mildly good at business math (or any math for that matter), and I learned how to do it in extremely hostile circumstances with almost no help. I had to figure it out on my own and if I did math or analysis of any kind wrong, I was shamed for it.

Still not convinced? Here are a few more facts that had zero impact on my ability to sustainably grow businesses:

- I was homeschooled and **barely** got past algebra.

- I got my GED to get into college and I'm pretty sure math was pass/fail.
- I didn't go to business school. I *applied* to the business program in undergrad and they rejected me. The letter suggested I apply for the school of arts, which I did!
- Revenue recognition is more complex in execution than you think, but I still can't explain exactly why.
- If I haven't made a spreadsheet in a while, I have to relearn the formulas and pivot table witchery I'd mastered before, and my report-building skills have not progressed beyond intermediate-level competency (though I've gotten really good at asking for help in this area!).

My point is, none of this mattered when it came to analyzing the performance of the agency and making it a multi-million ARR business. I figured it out! Data storytelling isn't a specialized skill that only certain people can master. Once you learn a cursory amount about very basic accounting and familiarize yourself with common reports that executives look at, you realize the simplicity of what they are communicating using fancy terminology and a lot of jargon. And when you learn just a little bit more, you will see how many people are acting like they are saying something of substance about the business when really they are saying nothing at all (or simply repeating something already stated).

Remember, getting good at reporting on marketing isn't about being a master mathematician or data analyst or excel expert. It's about understanding the larger business context surrounding your work and crafting a narrative that communicates the message you want delivered to whatever stakeholders are involved. So if you need to ask your data team to build you a spreadsheet and show you how it works, that makes you a strategic leader, not a dummy.

The reality is, most things in business that help you gain power and leverage are easier to learn than people already in power make it seem. The hard part is navigating around the corporate blah, blah, blah to build trust with the right people who can provide the knowledge and context you need to create reports your stakeholders can actually use.

This often comes at a cost, so bravery is crucial here. You are going to feel dumb sometimes, both on your own and because other people will make you feel that way. I've been uncomfortable throughout my career because I consistently put myself in situations where I'm out of my depth. The more you do that, the less often you are out of your depth and the more influential you become. But you'll suffer a bit along the way, and that's the truth. Sometimes unfairly so. I've been in countless humiliating situations that were unfair and wrong and every time it's absolutely horrible.

But I never let it stop me, and neither should you. Though I should clarify: To me, being brave about acquiring knowledge means you're willing to be out of your depth sometimes in order to obtain it. And that includes admitting you don't know things to people you're trying to impress in order to learn it. What bravery doesn't mean to me is allowing people to treat you disrespectfully. It's up to you to decide where that line is. Just know there *are* companies where you can learn and grow without being unduly punished along the way.

Alrighty? Let's get into it then.

KEY POINT

Advice from **Ann Handley**

My question is, how do you know it's *not* creating the action you want to inspire?

B2B content is part of a complex matrix of various touchpoints, seen and unseen, including word of mouth, dark social, that one guy who mentioned your brand on LinkedIn. B2B—or any marketing—is a less straightforward path; more conspiratorial crime scene investigation board.

What marketers can do about it is to rethink the messy muddle of attribution to think about more meaningful ways to determine what's "working."

Instead of just measuring how many people downloaded a white paper, look at how many people then signed up for your email newsletter. And then, how many of them wrote back to you when you told a story in the last issue about a specific problem they have? What did existing customers tell you worked the last time you spoke with them?

Rethink off-the-shelf metrics (because there is no shelf).[1]

Marketing Fundamentals: A Quick Review

Marketing can contribute to company growth in many different ways: net new sales, customer retention, reduces risk from competitors, sometimes creates new revenue streams (like events) that impact more than one company goal, bringing a product to market successfully, feature adoption/upsells, to name a few.

The challenge marketers have is convincing multiple stakeholders that their work did, in fact, contribute in any of these areas. Even if you have goals and agreed-upon metrics to measure success, reporting on marketing ends up being fraught with all kinds of complications, from the political and interpersonal to depth of knowledge about marketing and what shows up as "impact" and "value" to the business.

The opportunity for marketers in this situation is that the people who need to be convinced don't know what "the answer" to marketing attribution is either. They argue with each other about it behind closed doors and change their minds a lot, but they honestly can't really prove anything better than you can. They just bought into some corollary model or made one up and have spent a ton of time campaigning internally and out in the world to make other people believe their way is correct and eventually some of them do.

Numbers don't tell stories, people tell stories.

You're Not Reporting, You're Campaigning

Reporting on marketing can either be your undoing or a tool you use to retain support from stakeholders across the company who all have different motivations, POVs, and goals who might otherwise derail your plan. Think of reporting like a marketing campaign. It's a mix of behind-the-scenes campaigning to small groups and individuals, messaging from your marketing team, etc. throughout execution. By the time you share your official report, you should be reminding people of what you already said rather than sharing anything new.

The good news for marketers is that we're really good at this stuff already. We excel in crafting convincing narratives. Our specialty is researching and connecting seemingly disparate things together and speaking with authority about topics they just learned about and doing so well enough that actual experts publish it under their name. And all you need to be successful is a little context so you can be more strategic in your approach.

What Is the Purpose of Performance Reporting?

Reporting on marketing to stakeholders is less an act of honest reflection than it is a PR campaign. I'm not suggesting that you say anything that is untrue. What I'm saying is that the truth on its own, even when it's good, won't help you.

Even if your marketing initiatives outperformed your goals and expectations, don't wait until the end of a reporting period to share this information with them. The less they have to think about how marketing is performing the better it is for you, and the best way to direct their focus elsewhere is to bore them with regular updates where not much has changed and anticipate possible issues that may come up later.

There is no one right way to report on marketing. The right way ends up being whatever convinces the stakeholders you need in your corner that it's working. There are no best practices or logic that I can share with you, because those aren't always the things that convince people, including business leaders (though they will claim otherwise).

Instead, reporting is more an exercise in discovery through experimentation. It entails trial and error and a lot of imagination and storytelling. Think of it the same way you might test marketing tactics to see if they are effective at influencing potential customers. You're experimenting to see what resonates with the stakeholders you need to influence.

And, for what it's worth I still don't always get it right the first time. That's because you can't know a person's motivations, triggers, etc., right off the bat. I'm going to get you a little past the starting line with some principles and factors that are common, but in the end figuring out what to report on and how will depend almost entirely on the circumstances of your particular company, who you are reporting to, and your ability to build relationships with them.

What Do You Want?

When you think about reporting on marketing, it's best to begin by establishing what *you* want and how you're going to use the report to help you get it.

Setting a personal goal is crucial, for a few reasons. First, it ensures you're extracting personal value from your work beyond a paycheck. Whether marketing is your ultimate career goal doesn't matter. More skills = more options and many can be applied in more than one career category.

Second, it will motivate you to invest the time and effort to master this aspect of your job, which you'll need, because the trial and error involved is going to create some discomfort for you. There needs to be a payoff for you.

"It" could be as simple as, "I want my CEO to leave me alone." No matter what, weaving qualitative and quantitative data into a narrative about the impact of your work is one of the best ways to do that.

Remember: *If you're not working for yourself at work, other people will gain from you for free.*

Who Is the Report For?

Just because you're creating a report for your CMO doesn't mean they are the intended reader. Often, CMOs rely on their individual functional leads to provide a report that not only shows *them* you achieved your goals, but also serves as an example of their overall strategy working. The same is true regardless of who you're delivering the strategy to, so make sure you ask, but here's a rule of thumb:

- **CMO:** Use your report to make the case to the CEO and CFO that, even if the results aren't what they want, you are on top of it and therefore so is the CMO.

- **CEO:** Tell a really simple story because they aren't deep enough in the business for your context to be helpful to them. Also, don't hide the bad stuff; they know or will find out and it'll make them not trust you or think you don't know what you're talking about.

- **Client:** Make them look good to their boss

Who Else Is Going to Read It?

Are there other members of the board or C-suite with influence over executive decisions or (who are invisible decision-makers themselves) who will be reading your report? What about your team? Are there folks you need to strategically elevate or initiatives you need to call out to ensure your team is motivated and supported?

How Is Your Content Marketing Strategy Impacting the Business?

As you start thinking about what to include in your report, remember this:

> Both your boss and your CEO must show—with numbers—that marketing is working.

My recommendation: Learn how to produce a performance report demonstrating that marketing "works" based on your company's stated objectives as well as the unstated concerns and goals of your boss's boss.

This includes the "immeasurable" activities, too. I consider it part of a content marketer's job to produce narratives for their stakeholders that *they* understand and are excited to share. That's because marketing has always been about influencing the behavior of humans, which means marketing *strategy*, no matter what type of marketing you do, is only effective if it convinces the stakeholders who control whether it happens or not.

This is hard to do, given that the types of business impact leaders recognize as valuable are difficult to correlate with signals from marketing activities.

Perhaps most prescient: The people *your business leaders* report to operate on a completely different value paradigm, which means that most of their job consists of telling stories to stakeholders to get and maintain *their* buy-in. It's a very tricky balancing act, too, because your executive team must prove that the vision they set out to realize with this company is fulfilling their stakeholders' requirements while still delivering a valuable service or product to customers and creating an environment where people want to work.

Everyone has a boss.

I know what you're thinking and you are absolutely right: My explanation assumes that the folks leading your company actually care about their customers and team more than they care about profits, and that isn't always the case. It's also a grossly oversimplified version of the nuance that exists within every company. However, operating with the understanding that whomever you are reporting to has to report to someone else who is at least one giant step removed from your point of view is the most impactful advice I can give you. It puts you in a curious mindset, open to learning about how and what business leaders prioritize (without judgment), which enables you to craft performance reports that fulfill *their* objectives and thus yours too.

What Is the Format? How Much Time Do You Have?

Are you providing a five-minute update in a group Zoom call with the marketing team? Are you giving a presentation to your CMO? Are you sharing a written update to the entire company?

Regardless of the format, time, or length, I suggest you create your reports assuming that the person you need to read this the most (your boss or the CEO—or both) will only skim the first page. And even if they do read the second or third or the whole thing (doubtful, rare) the odds of them retaining more than one or two things are unlikely, so you need to make sure that first page is entirely focused on those one or two things.

If you don't, your CEO will conclude their own takeaways and they will likely be taken out of context, won't be accurate, and become the foundation of a new belief the entire company has about marketing.

How Often Are You Required to Provide This Report?

If this is a recurring report, make sure to connect the dots period-over-period to ensure the person you're reporting to sees the bigger picture. Don't assume they will remember anything about your last report or even if they do that they will make the necessary connections. They're pulled in 100 different directions—do the work for them, tell the story *you* want to tell.

How Often Does It Make Sense to Share Performance Updates to Achieve the Outcomes You Established?

This is where you apply strategy to your requirements. Based on the information you gather and the hypothesis you develop, create report types and comms schedules that serve your desired outcomes and see what happens. If you can maintain objectivity here, you'll learn quickly and even leverage the process itself to build stronger relationships with your stakeholders.

THE COMMUNITY MEASUREMENT FRAMEWORK

Jeff Bull, *Head of Developer Community and Strategy*

An adaptable framework that provides clear answers to two critical questions:

1 Is our community growing in meaningful ways?

2 Are we investing in the right places to nurture that growth?

While the specific tools and point values might change, the core concept works for any community:

1 Define what actions truly matter for your business.

2 Weight those actions based on their impact.

3 Track trends over time.

4 Correlate with business outcomes.

This framework gives you the high-level metrics executives want and transforms community building from a "feel-good" activity into a measurable driver of business growth. It also provides a wealth of insights to use elsewhere in your content marketing and to continue improving your community approach over time.

The goal isn't perfect measurement. It's having enough signal to make better decisions about where and how to invest in your community. "Sometimes the most valuable metric is the one that prompts the right questions rather than providing all the answers."

Common Reporting Mistakes Marketers Make

Reporting Activities, Not Outcomes

I see this mistake constantly, especially with marketing teams desperate to prove their worth to executives who don't understand marketing fundamentals. They present impressive stats on content volume, publishing cadence, and social media posts created—all activity metrics that executives couldn't care less about. Activity doesn't equal impact. Your CEO and board aren't interested in how many blog posts you published; they want to know how those posts influenced pipeline generation, shortened sales cycles, or reduced customer acquisition costs. When I became CEO of Animalz, I immediately scrapped our activity-based reporting and redirected our focus to client outcomes. The shift wasn't easy, but it transformed how we communicated value both internally and to clients, ultimately helping us grow from $3 million to $12 million in just over two years.

Letting Data Tell the Story

So many marketers dump raw analytics into a slide deck, point to a graph with an upward trend, and expect executives to connect the dots themselves. When I consult with clients, I often see 20-slide decks filled with website traffic charts, channel breakdowns, and engagement metrics—with zero narrative connecting this data to business outcomes. This approach leaves your audience thinking, "So what?" It's your job to interpret the data and explicitly show how your content efforts contributed to business goals. For example, don't just report that organic traffic increased 40 percent; explain that this traffic spike generated 25 percent more demo requests, resulting in $50K of new pipeline from prospects who wouldn't have found you otherwise. The story matters more than the numbers.

Using Too Much Jargon

Marketing teams love their specialized vocabulary—MPAs, TOFUs, attribution models, and conversion funnels. When presenting to non-marketing executives, this language creates an immediate disconnect. I once watched a CMO lose a budget approval because they spent 15 minutes explaining their sophisticated multi-touch attribution model instead of simply showing how content influenced revenue. Your CFO doesn't need to understand your SEO strategy's technical details; they need to know how that strategy delivers financial results. When I report to executives, I ruthlessly eliminate marketing jargon. I focus on business outcomes using language that resonates with finance, sales, and product teams. This translation work isn't optional—it's essential for gaining cross-functional support.

Failing to Provide Context

Numbers without context are meaningless. Is a 3 percent conversion rate good or bad? Did that 15 percent traffic increase meet expectations? Without benchmarks and context, your reporting leaves stakeholders unable to interpret your results. Providing proper context prevents folks from drawing incorrect conclusions and helps build confidence in your strategy, even when certain metrics might not look impressive in isolation.

Be careful not to lean into industry benchmarks too much or at all. Ideally you're creating your own benchmarks based on your growth goals, activities, audience behavior, etc.

PRO TIPS

1 Don't tell them what you did, tell them what you accomplished.

2 Show how what you accomplished impacts company objectives (even if it's not direct)—make this simple.

3 Extras/bonus: If something unexpected happened or you tried something, even if it didn't work, if you express it clearly, simply, and reflect on learning and say what's next (in four sentences), they will like it.

4 Keep it simple: It's ok to have tons of detail, just don't include it all. Put it in the Appendix so they can refer to it if they want to.

5 Try not to compare. There are some leaders who obsess over competition. They want to know what their competitors are up to. This is not a good way to benchmark whether you're doing a good job or not. There's a whole bunch of variables that you can't see that could be driving their success. This may not convince your CEO, but it's important for you not to encourage it.

6 Be specific: Don't use jargon words or terms. It makes you look junior. Say exactly what you mean.

7 Highlight efficiencies: Where were you clever in ideas and execution that compounded results or saved money?

Remember: Everything is made up, including reports, so the better you understand the stuff you're reporting on, the more you can use it to get what YOU want, too!

Signal vs. Noise: Predicting Future Impact

Most reporting focuses on what's already happened—last month's lead generation, last quarter's revenue, or last year's customer acquisition costs.

While historical data is crucial to making future decisions, it also keeps marketing leaders in a reactive position. By the time you identify a problem, it's already affected your results. Leading indicators give you time to adjust course when needed, rather than explaining missed targets after the fact.

That's why monitoring the signals along the way is also useful, if executed thoughtfully.

A few caveats:

- **Monitor quietly.** You don't have to share what you observe with your executives 1) at all, or 2) until you're ready. They'll either get confused or too excited, and neither leads to a good place for you.

- **Work with your data team.** Whatever job title they've been given at your company, find the people who have access to the raw data and ask them questions. Be specific about what you want to know. You don't have to know the exact data types, time periods, or segments. They just need a detailed *question* to get you what you need.

- **Talk it through.** Since data contains multiple realities depending how you slice it, I've always found it helpful to run any conclusions or stories by my data team and, where possible, my boss (see first bullet!). Basically, I look for two different analytical perspectives:

  - someone whose job it is to ensure our data is accurate
  - someone whose job it is to analyze data for reporting on the business

Remember: Reporting isn't a single use-case activity. Reflecting on the past to measure impact is just one way to leverage reporting. Use it to inspire new ideas, optimizations, and experiments, too.

A Few Potentially Useful Signals You Can Monitor

Ultimately, it's up to you to determine which signals provide valuable insights into the performance of your marketing initiatives. And regardless of your role, whether it's producer, manager, or team lead, as your boss, I'd expect you to know how to determine what those are.

Also, the exact signals you monitor will continue to change as technology and the internet evolve. However, there are a few informative signals that have stood the test of time (thus far) for me.

RESONANCE

When it comes to resonance, unprompted action on even a semi-regular basis is a huge signal that something you're doing is working, so even if your data is statistically insignificant, I'd lean in and at the very least conduct further experiments.

One example of this is folks sharing and referencing a topic or idea you share publicly in their own content (and how their followers react to it) on a semi-consistent basis. This indicates you're at least on the right track with content direction.

In my experience, search volume for a keyword or phrase is minimally helpful to determining resonance in the beginning. As in, just because no one is searching for a topic doesn't mean it's not a common problem. A more useful exercise in search monitoring to me is whether your campaign corresponds with an increase in search volume in that time period.

ACTIVITY

The same principle applies to other actions as well.

Are folks commenting on posts asking for your opinion on specific problems they are experiencing? Are you receiving anecdotal feedback semi-consistently on specific marketing initiatives or topics you're investing in?

Do folks engage with your content even when you're inconsistent? One client I worked with saw 60–70 percent open rates even on major holidays or when the newsletter was sent off-schedule on a Saturday or Monday.

Are you seeing an increase in time-on-page or pages per session from certain topics or even specific pieces?

COPYCATS

While not a perfect signal, if your competitors start copying your content, it's either a sign you could be onto something or an indication that their strategy isn't working, they don't have one, or they're struggling. No matter the case, it's a signal worth paying attention to and perhaps doing some recon to find out if there are any weaknesses you can exploit.

Ultimately, your goal is to explore these signals to establish whether there are correlations between these leading indicators and your ultimate business outcomes. This isn't just theoretical—it requires analyzing your data to identify patterns that predict success for your business.

Conclusion: Turning Measurement Into Mastery

Effective reporting isn't the end of your marketing journey—it's the bridge to your next phase of growth. Measuring the impact of content marketing isn't just about proving its value; it's about creating the leverage you need to execute strategies that genuinely move your business forward.

Remember these essential principles as you develop your measurement approach:

- **Numbers don't tell stories—people do.** Your data provides ingredients, but you create the meal. The most powerful reports transform complex metrics into clear narratives that inspire action and build confidence in your strategy.

- **Measurement serves strategy, not the other way around.** When you begin with clear objectives and understand what truly influences behavior, metrics become tools for insight rather than constraints on creativity.

- **Reporting is campaigning.** The most successful marketers recognize that performance reporting is ultimately a persuasion exercise— one that requires understanding audience motivations, building relationships, and consistently communicating value.

- **Both measurable and unmeasurable impacts matter.** While focusing on quantifiable metrics, never lose sight of the equally valuable but harder-to-measure effects of brand building, relationship development, and community growth.

By developing measurement systems that capture both immediate impacts and leading indicators, you transform reporting from a dreaded obligation into a strategic advantage.

As you apply these principles to your own marketing, remember that mastery comes through practice and persistence. You'll make mistakes, discover unexpected insights, and continuously refine your approach. That's not just normal—it's the path to excellence.

Note

1 Total Anarchy" a newsletter by Ann Handley: AnnHandley.com/newsletter (archived at https://perma.cc/N7XU-2RV9)

10

What Makes *Good* Content?

Have you ever seen a baby when it first comes out?

I have, and they're not cute at all. They're slimy, screaming, and covered in their own excrement (and sometimes their mom's too). But with a few helping hands from midwives, nurses, doctors, they become soooo cute.

Ideas are a lot like newborn babies. They are definitely rough around the edges at first, but you love your ugly little ideas because they're yours. However, unlike a newborn baby, it is precisely because it's your idea that you should not fall in love with it.

This may sound counterintuitive but often the best way to help your idea develop and thrive is to be critical of it. Good content doesn't often emerge fully formed. Which brings us to the question at the heart of this chapter: What actually makes content good?

What Exactly Is *Quality* Content?

Everyone talks about "quality content," but no one seems to agree on what that actually means. The truth is there is no universal definition of quality. A strategic approach to quality is to create your own definition based largely on what your customer likes.

In the meantime, here are three definitions I believe in (obviously one of them is my own!):

How I Define Quality Content

Quality isn't safe; it's daring. It's hard to copy. If you feel uncomfortable, you're on the right track. If you're exuberant and you also feel a strong impulse to run in the opposite direction, it's time to share it:

- surprising
- teaches me something new
- changes how I think
- entertaining

Does your customer think it's good?

Notice I didn't say "solve customer pain point" or anything more specific (although that is also another measurement of "quality" as you'll see below). But did they like it and have a good experience?

Did it achieve your intended outcome?

Or did it lead to an idea that achieved your intended outcome?

You don't always need to create new ideas.

Developing existing ideas deeper, in new ways, is also "quality." E.g. repurposing, reaction vids, riffing on another person's idea (this is also a strategy re getting them to share).

Great Content Helps People

Wil Reynolds, founder and CEO of Seer Interactive, and someone who was a huge inspiration to me in my career, says it like this: "Helpful content gets shared in places that are very hard to track (email, WhatsApp, LinkedIn, Facebook Groups, etc.), but where there are trusted people who filter the value from the noise. It uplifts the perception of the brand—we remember the helpers. Sometimes it's better to write content that doesn't rank than mediocre content that does."

The Universal Quality Bar

Robyn Showers, a brand and marketing expert who's built content programs at companies like HubSpot, Vimeo, and Apollo has a three-part definition:

- **It has to have a purpose.** For B2B content, it's about being useful. For consumer-focused content, it's more about being entertaining.

In both cases, the content needs to serve a purpose. It needs to do something internally and externally, it has to actually provide some kind of value. It has to solve a real problem for the audience, even if it's a small problem.

- **It has to be original,** meaning it has to add something to the conversation. If it's just a rehash of other people's thoughts, it has to add something new, like framing it in a way that is clearer, more succinct, or easier to digest. It has to do something that other articles or other videos out there aren't doing.

- **It has to be delightful,** even if it's just the delight in the authenticity of the person or the brand. Maybe the delight is that it's funny. Something about it has to leave a positive impression on the person who watches it or reads it

There's No Single Definition of Quality and It's Fine

Three different—and successful—people in content marketing all define quality a little differently. *So what?*

Quality means different things to different people. Even the dictionary description is vague to the point of being absurd: "The standard of something as measured against other things of a similar kind; the degree of excellence of something."

Think about the listicle. This is one of the most commonly used types of blog post content marketers use, even though most of them hate it, but they continue to publish them because they are popular among readers.

What about video? For years, you needed big budgets to create videos, but now a person talking to their phone camera with text over it performs just as well. Both could be considered "quality."

Sometimes quality is the idea itself, rather than the way it's presented. Other times, the idea matters less than how it's presented.

LinkedIn is a good example of this. When I first started publishing posts, "quality" to me included a healthy dose of creativity that my friends loved but didn't really fit the platform. At the time I didn't care, but when I was ready to build an audience I hired Christine

Orchard, a LinkedIn strategist, and she taught me how to restructure my posts to get more attention while saying the same thing. Within two months my posts started going viral and I gained 2,000 new followers.

My point is, stop worrying about THE definition and create your own meaning of quality. Just make sure your criteria match what your audience recognizes as quality too!

The Problem with Quality as a North Star

One of the biggest mistakes I made and I see marketing teams make is focusing too heavily on content quality as the driving factor of their programs' success. I saw this repeatedly during my time at Animalz, where clients would obsess over making every piece perfect while missing larger strategic opportunities. Here's why this is problematic.

Quality is inherently subjective and constantly evolving based on changes in:

- human behavior
- technological advancements
- cultural movements
- community preferences

To make your content "high quality" you need to know your customer and design with them at core and contextualize so they remember it's what they want.

Speak in their language. Grammar doesn't matter to everyone and can turn certain people off because it appears too contrived.

Companies often treat quality as a static target, creating rigid:

- style guides
- communication guidelines
- brand standards

- marketing ops processes
- customer profiles

This leads them to miss opportunities that could give them unique advantages. They get stuck in the "should" trap:

- we should be on social media
- we should have a podcast
- we should be creating video content

Should you?

The result: Companies adopt performance metrics that don't impact their ultimate growth goals.

TIP

You need a new bit.

Here's a hard truth that many marketers don't want to hear: Creating "quality" content is the minimum barrier to entry, not a competitive advantage. If your content isn't good, buyers will simply use one of the countless other options available to them.

TOOLS HAVE DEMOCRATIZED QUALITY

It's easier than ever to produce consistently good content thanks to:

- WYSIWYG editors that enforce good design principles
- tools like Canva that automatically optimize image ratios
- AI writing assistants that help with grammar and style
- analytics tools that provide immediate feedback on performance

The early mover advantage window is closed. Content marketing is mainstream and has been for a while. Companies that first leveraged search as a discovery channel had a unique advantage. Then it was companies using long-form content. Then it was structured content for search. Each wave of innovation provided temporary advantages, but those advantages were eventually copied and neutralized.

Time for content marketers to write a new hit song.

We're no longer spending time convincing companies to do content marketing—everyone's already doing it. The conversation has shifted from "should we do content marketing?" to "how do we do it better?"

Who Really Determines What's Quality Anyway?

This happened a lot at the agency: Our editors were satisfied with the quality of a piece and the client wasn't. Sometimes everyone was happy and it performed well and I thought the article was lame.

Creating client content by applying our definition of quality didn't make all our customers happy, because they didn't always recognize it.

Achieving "quality" our customers would recognize required relationship management more than anything else:

- understanding their vision of quality to build the trust required to continue working with them, deepen our relationship, and produce better work;
- getting them to publish anything at all to show value in the form of performance metrics, so continue working with them, deepen our relationship, and produce better work.

When I ran content at Help Scout, they were meticulous—almost maniacal—about making every single piece of content perfect. I used to get anxiety before we posted anything, fearing there was an error I missed or the CEO wouldn't like it. Still, I loved their obsession with perfection; it was a form of indulgence in craft that made me proud of the work we did.

But time and again, when I looked at which blog posts, emails, campaigns, contributed the most to our team's goal (traffic), they weren't the ones we spent the most time on. They weren't the ones with beautiful new illustrations or a gorgeous UX our cofounder and lead designer made just for that one piece.

The content that drove the most traffic—by a large margin—was things like updating specific parts of old SEO blog posts that had fallen in SERP rankings. But, of course, we couldn't update them too much, otherwise we'd disappear from the first page altogether. I recall making substantive updates to our highest-traffic post, which brought in something like 100k visitors per month. The information in it was vague; it needed more examples. It wasn't "good quality" anymore.

After making substantive edits to the post and republishing, our traffic tanked, and we had to revert back to the original version.

Which version was better?

To me, it was the updated version. To Google, it was the old version that, objectively wasn't as helpful as the updated version. Now, this was in 2016 when Google's search algorithm was in a different state of development, but still!

My point is that what I think are the criteria for quality content doesn't really matter. It's technically irrelevant. Because quality is in the eye of the beholder, in platform rules or community guidelines, in algorithms, in cultural norms, trends, zeitgeist, whatever you want to call it. Criteria for quality content change over time, including the most fundamental components like grammar, punctuation, pronouns, vocabulary.

But I know you aren't going to give up the question... even knowing it can be subjective and a moving target, how, then, do you create quality content??

Developing Quality B2B Content Marketing

Since there isn't a universal definition of quality, I can't give you THE answer, but it would be rude to have a chapter on quality and leave you with nothing. Here's how I evaluate the value and efficacy of B2B content marketing:

- **Is it serving company goals?*** This is an indication that it's working for your audience, too, since your company goals should center on the customer.

- **Can you execute on it?** People, resources etc. you need are available to you when you need them.

- **Can you sustain what's working?** In other words, can you execute it long enough for it to show results?

Serving business goals with content is part of the creative process! It's not just about words and pictures and CTAs—it's about strategy and the ability to execute it too. Because if you can't execute, then it's not good and you have to come up with another idea.

If you want to achieve maximum ROI on your content marketing strategy, you need to have space to play, experiment, learn, refine. Then rinse, repeat. This is how new forms of virality are uncovered. This is how some brands are "made" while others fade away.

It's All About Your Audience

The only person whose opinion matters about quality is the person whose attention you're trying to get. And that attention can take unexpected forms. Surprise, a sense of urgency, loneliness, anger: These are all forms of getting attention and can be "high quality" parts of your strategy if they lead to your intended outcome.

Remember: Your uniqueness is your competitive advantage–no one else has your exact perspective or style. More often than not, the things that make you unique are higher leverage than conforming to industry norms. There are infinite ways to tell the same story, and to discover new angles—you need only to look to your customers, your team, and yourself.

Just make sure to be selective about details. Literature uses vivid descriptions to immerse readers; business content should do the opposite. Spark curiosity so they want to learn more—don't give them everything upfront.

How Do I Know If I'm Successful?

I can't tell you exactly what to do to achieve quality content, but I can tell you what not to do: *Don't do what everyone else is doing.*

Instead, look for some of these signals:

- the community saying your messaging back to you, to each other, externally;

- sharing aspects of your vision and how it impacts them externally and internally;
- the community offering their own ideas based on the messaging and ideas you've shared.

Conclusion: Defining Quality on Your Own Terms

There is no universal standard for quality that applies across all contexts, audiences, and business goals.

This realization isn't a limitation—it's liberating. It means you get to define quality based on what works for your audience and business, rather than chasing an abstract ideal that might not serve either one.

Here are what I think are the most important takeaways I can leave you with, but keep in mind that this is just my opinion!

- **Quality is relative and constantly evolving.** What works today may not work tomorrow. What resonates with one audience segment might fall flat with another. Embrace this fluidity rather than fighting it.
- **Your audience is the ultimate arbiter of quality.** Neither your personal preferences, your CEO's opinions, nor industry best practices matter if your content doesn't connect with the people you're trying to reach. Watch what they engage with, share, and implement—that's your real quality metric.
- **"Good" content achieves its purpose.** A piece that drives massive conversion with minimal production value is objectively better than a perfectly polished asset that generates no results. Define success by outcomes, not inputs.
- **Experimentation is essential.** The only way to discover what quality means for your audience is to try different approaches, analyze the results, and refine accordingly. Set aside time and resources for play, exploration, and learning.
- **Tools have democratized technical quality.** With today's technology, even small teams can produce content that meets basic professional

standards. Your competitive advantage comes from unique perspectives, authentic voices, and strategic alignment—not production polish.

Sometimes the most effective content breaks the rules that even you have set. Your willingness to challenge conventions could be your greatest competitive advantage.

Most importantly: No more "should" content, ok?

In the next chapter, we'll explore how to secure buy-in for your content marketing strategy—including how to help stakeholders understand this more nuanced view of quality that prioritizes results over rigid standards.

11

Securing Buy-in for Your Content Marketing Strategy

Funny story: most of the marketing skills you worked so hard to develop? Completely useless once you hit senior leadership.

I learned this lesson by believing I was "doing leadership" perfectly and thinking I was smarter than my bosses when it was obvious I was making rookie mistakes.

One of my favorite fall-on-my-face moments was when the head of product at a startup I worked for explained the difference between a plan and a strategy to me, and I didn't get it at all.

The president, who I reported to, left the company suddenly and the head of product was my new boss. We had just released a new product and he asked me to create a product marketing strategy to increase adoption among our user base (or something like that, I honestly don't remember). This was my second marketing role ever, my first role as a marketing *manager*, and the totality of my marketing experience was less than a year.

Naturally, I couldn't wait to show off my elite marketing skills.

I pulled out the markers, wrote things on whiteboards and pieces of paper that I taped all over the conference room. I made *connections*. I had *ideas*. I stayed late, smoking cigarettes on the stoop when I needed a break from my brilliant thoughts.

Devin Bramhall's Very First Content Marketing Strategy™ contained the types of content I would create, distribution plans, a publishing calendar, how and when I would execute every part. There were emails to be sent, timelines to follow, goals to hit. I couldn't wait to share it with him.

When I finished presenting it to him, I had a huge smile on my face as I waited for his praise.

"This is a great plan, but what's your strategy?" he replied.

"This is my strategy," I said, assuming it was *his* misunderstanding and not my lack of knowledge.

I'll spare you the 30-minute back and forth during which my head of product delicately tried to explain to me that a list of activities, organized in chronological order with detailed steps and task assignments is not, in fact, a strategy.

It's a plan.

A strategy, he tried to explain, is a solution. It includes an execution plan, but the approach is what achieves the objective. Like how content marketing was a solution for B2B Saas companies that needed to grow fast but experienced longer sales cycles than their consumer marketing brethren.

That's the solution my head of product was looking for, and I completely missed it.

Making More Pizza vs. Making More Profit

He wasn't interested in how I made the pizza. He wanted to know my approach for increasing the volume of pizzas we could make and distribute during prime dinner hours by 25 percent while only increasing costs by a maximum of 5 percent. To give him confidence, all I needed to show him was which puzzle pieces I would use and how I would fit them together to produce the outcome he was looking for. He didn't need the pizza recipes or staff schedules. Instead, he wanted me to show him something like:

- Analyze the last three months of orders to determine the three to five most popular pizza types. Create a dedicated assembly counter stocked with a volume of ingredients to match the higher average volume of those pizza types.

- Hire one additional part-time staff member to work Friday–Sunday just prepping pizza dough, enabling us to accommodate x percent more orders during the busiest days of the week. We already have a few part-time folks from the local high school and adding another won't increase costs by much.

- Evaluate order volume after the first weekend executing this new plan to see if we shipped more, less, or the same number of pizzas. Also, speak with staff to learn what worked and what didn't, so we can make some quick improvements before the following weekend.

- Continue this cycle for four weeks then analyze the order and revenue data, food, and any other costs associated with making and delivering pizzas, plus feedback from staff and customers to understand whether the approach shows improvement (or signals that it's working) or if we need to go in another direction.

(Note: I have never actually worked in a pizza shop, so don't try this at home.)

It was only years later when I was a fresh-faced CEO that I finally realized what he was talking about.

A Peek Inside the CEO Mindset

One of our managers at the agency approached my COO with an idea for a new content service we could provide and wanted to pitch me on it. My COO asked me if I would give this manager 30 minutes to pitch me and I agreed, asking the manager to send me a one-page explainer beforehand so I could orient myself ahead of the meeting.

To this day, I don't remember the idea the manager pitched. I can't even remember which manager it was. Other folks pitched ideas to me that I remember, even if we didn't do them, but my only memories of this encounter were the mistakes the person made.

First, their write-up contained too much information. There were a lot of details about what the service was and how we'd execute it, which are important once it's time to execute, but unnecessary when you're trying to sell an executive on an idea.

If you want me to lean into your idea, it needs to be easy to understand and the value has to hit me over the head. It should be like an "aha" moment where you're connecting two things that have been in plain sight to me all along, I just never saw how they went together.

And remember, bogging me down in operational details makes me depressed at this point in the buy-in journey. I want to know you've thought of them and can speak to obvious potential challenges, but I don't expect you to have them all solved, and if you're honest about identifying it and not researching it yet, I'll see that as good prioritization. Especially if you've hit me over the head with a value proposition that doesn't take any effort for me to see.

Another helpful consideration is ease of execution. If you want me to say yes to your strategy or your idea, then pitch me something that is an easy-to-do, solves a short-term problem that I've already talked about recently, and is, like, the main problem I'm focused on right now. Most importantly: Don't make me do any work. Handle it. If you need me to do anything at all then the odds of it happening even if I say yes are slim. Otherwise, your idea has to be so groundbreaking that the amount of work it will take doesn't matter to me.

If not, consider timing as a factor for getting me to buy in. If you present a good idea at a bad time for me, it's not going to happen anyway. Be strategic! A lot of times it's better to pitch other managers and get buy-in elsewhere on the team if you want to make something happen.

In fact, the best piece of advice I can give you is to go to the CEO last with your ideas. If we like it and go to the exec team with it, they're going to be pissed that you distracted me. Distracted leaders like shiny things and it drives their exec team crazy. Good leaders are skeptical of changing course on a dime, because they do the math on the cost of changing course while mid-journey. Take that into account.

If you do a bad job pitching me, you're going to leave a bad impression on me, sorry. Especially if you haven't done a basic Google search to see what already exists. I need to see that you care enough about your own idea to do the work before pitching me, otherwise why should I care?

> TIP
>
> The "new thing" category is what folks pitched me on the most and none of the ideas were actually new, they were just new to the person pitching me. Do your homework! If a version of it already exists and you haven't factored that in already as part of the reason you're pitching this idea, then you need to do more research and analysis.
>
> Whatever you pitch, it needs to be significantly *better* than anything we're doing right now for me to want to consider it, and that's a tough bar to clear, but it also shouldn't stop you.
>
> I've had a lot of ideas in my career that I thought were awesome and most of them weren't and it's fine! I'm not saying don't pitch them, you definitely should, even if your idea sucks. You'll learn more about what makes a good idea and also hone your pitching skills. What I'm saying is that before you fall in love with your idea, you need to tear it apart like someone who hates the idea first and here's why:
>
> - you'll either be more passionate about the idea or you'll see that it's no good and free your mind to brainstorm in another direction;
> - you'll surface obstacles to your idea that I'm definitely going to think of right away and ask you about when you pitch me on it;
> - you'll develop super useful analytical skills and learn more about how businesses work and your ideas will get so much better!
>
> If you don't do that before pitching your CEO or your boss on it then you're going to leave a conversation with me frustrated, because our questions are valid and if you didn't know to think of them, then you didn't do your basic homework before pitching the idea. That's on you!

Important distinction here: There's a difference between a lazy, unresearched pitch and an idea that I don't say yes to.

I loved when folks pitched me on their ideas, even though most of them weren't that interesting. It was an opportunity for me to coach and encourage them. Most often, I would ask them to gather additional information or work through a blocker I identified and come back to me. Less than 1 percent of them ever followed through, which is an opportunity for you!

My point is, the impression you leave by pitching me a bad idea *well* is extremely positive, so don't worry about being rejected. Have ideas, share ideas! Looking back, the idea itself mattered less than what I learned by pursuing it. I learned how to take feedback better, how to make a winnable case for my ideas, how to manage up, etc.

So, as we go into getting buy-in, just remember to pay attention to everything that happens throughout the process and try to extract every bit of learning and opportunity you can here. The folks I invested in were the ones who showed up, were curious, and took ownership of pursuing the idea. They didn't stop pitching ideas just because I said no to them. They returned to me with answers to my questions.

This is the same journey you'll be on with getting buy-in throughout your career. It's the same as pitching an idea. If you want me to say yes, make it easy for me (or whoever you're pitching). Don't share the details YOU want me to know, share the details I want to know. Find out, before you pitch what I'm worried about, how I best take in information and like being communicated to.

The truth is, if you invest heavily in educating yourself on the weird, illogical, and often unfair realities of the workplace then practice a lot, take feedback and learn, you're likely going to get good enough that you can get even a bad idea approved.

THE COMMON GROUND FRAMEWORK

I learned a TON about getting buy-in from my boss, the CMO at Help Scout, Suneet Bhatt. To this day I still affectionately call him "boss." He developed an alignment that I've found particularly effective:

1 **Start with common ground**
   - Find areas of agreement rather than focusing on differences
   - Build bridges from existing values to new initiatives
   - Look for shared priorities that can unite different teams

2 **Reframe rather than impose**
   - Position new initiatives in terms that resonate with existing culture

- Connect initiatives to core company values and priorities
- Example: Reframing "marketing" as "customer growth" to align with customer-centric culture

3 Protect and nurture new initiatives

- Build confidence through small wins before facing broader scrutiny
- Create safe spaces for teams to experiment and prove concepts
- Shield early efforts from harsh criticism while building momentum
- Understand executive motivations

So, What Changed?

It wasn't that I stopped caring about craft, quality, the depth of analysis, and finding more ways to experiment.

It was the *way* I cared about those things that changed. For example, I worried whether the way we'd leaned too heavily on SEO content and built processes to keep up with post-pandemic demand was putting the company at risk by narrowing our offer to one small facet of content marketing.

When it came to the day-to-day, I relied on my executive team to use the values and vision I'd set to ensure we remained on track toward our company goals and our mission. My job was the health of the entire business, which meant my priorities—and concerns— were abstracts of the individual challenges inside. It was my executive team working through the leaders they hired to manage nooks and crannies of the company then share—ideally preemptively—emerging issues and themes I needed to think about or find solutions for.

Also, the questions I asked were simpler:

- Did you do it or not? ("It" meaning an objective, a project, a deliverable.)
- What happened?
- What are you going to do now?

What makes those questions hard to answer for new managers is that you don't always know the criteria I'm looking for, so you default to sharing lots of detail, because you think that proves you know what you're doing when to me it shows you don't. At least the part that matters to me, which is the executive functioning part of your job.

Here are those questions again paired with answers I'm looking for.

Did You Do It or Not?

The answer CEO Devin is looking for is truly a yes/no followed by *only* the amount of context I've included below in the example (I'll explain why in a second). It sounds counterintuitive, but you help CEO Devin more by letting me ask you simple questions and take in information one piece at a time at first. Even as a content marketing CEO who deeply understood what our content managers were talking about, I wasn't immersed as deeply in the individual teams or their clients. Also, it's most likely my 145th context switch that day, so asking me to quickly go from high-level across the organization to deep into departmental performance or a client issue is like asking me to jump down an elevator shaft and land on my feet. Which means that, if you want to build trust with me, I just need you to answer my question directly and clearly. Here are examples of what I'm looking for:

Yes, we...

- ... hit our goal
- ... exceeded our goal by x percent
- ... missed our goal by x percent

Yes, but we...

... only completed x percent of the project, campaign, initiative and [insert one of the answers above].

No because...

- ... we were assigned a new objective that this marketing activity does not serve
- ... company strategy changed and we updated our plans to serve the new direction
- ... the new CMO* deprioritized it and gave us a new direction to follow

- ... we didn't need to because this other thing we did outperformed our expectations, so we changed course to invest more in that

Or whoever the decision-maker was, even if they are the ones asking the questions—just make sure you check your attitude at the door in your delivery.

What Happened?

For this question, I'm looking for two pieces of information (without telling you that when I ask the question, sorry):

- Did you achieve the goal and/or the outcomes you estimated? Why/why not?
- Did anything surprising happen that would be strategically beneficial or pertinent for me to know?

This one has another layer of complexity because, in addition to not verbalizing this question and expecting you to intuit that this is part of what I mean by "What happened?" I also expect you to know that there are only two correct ways to answer this question:

- no surprises, we are on track to hit our goals, or
- yes, here is an interesting stat or quote from a customer—any small dopamine hit I'll be excited to share on calls but is either neutral or positive in its impact.

Tread carefully with the "yes" answer, because you don't want it to agitate me into taking any kind of action. If the info makes me too interested, I'll meddle. If it makes me worry, I'll meddle. It's far better to say "it's all fine" or even "we got off to a bumpy start, but we're on track now" than risk sharing information that will make me get involved. Because the truth is, as much as you don't want me involved, I don't want to get involved either. But I will if I feel like it's "necessary" (i.e. I feel like you aren't managing it well or are focusing on the wrong success indicators). Here are a few examples:

The influencer campaign you launched brought in 1,000 new customers in the first week. (One thousand being any number that is so high it's an outlier and can't logically be repeated ever or anytime soon.) I'm so surprised and delighted that my body spontaneously produces a new gene called "Expectations" and the bar is set at 1,000 until I die. Truly. I will remember this moment for the rest of my life and no matter what qualifying logic you share with that number, my Expectations gene blocks me from hearing it. This is what I would call a rookie move. Surprise and delight aren't how you win the CEO over; it's a way to make yourself memorable to me in a positive way.

The LinkedIn portion of the campaign isn't contributing the way we thought it would, because while folks are watching and liking the videos, they aren't following through on the CTA. This is a can of live, smelly worms that ruins everyone's day, because it provokes a stream of unhelpful questions that I want answers to right away and if you don't have answers during the conversation we are in, I'm going to be annoyed and ask you to write up a "mini" report containing a summary of the entire campaign, every activity, and how much each activity is contributing to the goal, plus a comparison against our past three campaigns (whether or not they are similar or served the same goals) and how other companies have run the same campaign to understand what went wrong (I might even ask you to do this even if you know the answer without doing that research). Then I'm going to your boss to ask why they think the LinkedIn part of the campaign isn't working and what do they think we should be doing, and do we have the right team and well I've never thought we should invest in LinkedIn anyway, and I'd like a comprehensive analysis of all the marketing we've ever done and let's sit down next week and go through it line-by-line together, so I can "help" you (even though you already solved whatever the problem was and just told me you're launching updated material tomorrow. I'll probably even tell you to hold off launching the new campaign until we have that meeting next week).

What Are You Going to Do Now?

Here again, I'm really asking you more than one question and each one should be answered a little differently:

What is your new strategic direction?
I want a short, high-level answer to this question, along the lines of,
"I'm serving dinner next, because it's the time when we eat dinner."

What did you learn? In light of that, what are you going to change or keep the same?

I want to know things like if you're going to change your approach, your ICP, use different messaging, or implement a new way of measuring success. It's a version of "if this, then that." Because x happened, we are going to do y next. Still, keep it short and add minimal context—just a little bit more than the first answer.

Do you see mistakes you made and are you going to take responsibility for them?

Owning your mistakes, understanding why they happened, and objectively sharing next steps builds trust. Things go wrong, you make mistakes, ideas don't pan out. Those are the best times to win over management. Curiosity in understanding what went wrong, bravery in owning your part—sometimes you can win more trust in these situations than if things had gone to plan!

BUY-IN BLOCKERS: THE 5 WHYS

1 **Why is it hard to get marketing approved by the C-suite?**
   It's risky. There's no guarantee what you do will work and it *really* needs to work. What most executives and boards are unknowingly anxious about is the fact that they have to deputize the most important part of the business—making money—to a department and practice most of them do not fundamentally understand.

2 **Why don't decision-makers understand marketing?**
   The reason they don't understand marketing in the first place isn't that important. The problem you encounter more often is that they think they do, which means not only do they lack core marketing knowledge but most never become educated because they're convinced they are already experts.

3 **Why is marketing perceived as non-essential?**
   Businesses run on certainty, and many marketing activities lack the immediate, clear-cut ROI that other departments can demonstrate.

4 **Why do marketing outcomes seem intangible compared to financial metrics?**
   You're working with humans and emotions and, to my knowledge, there isn't software that tracks all human emotions and translates them into marketing impact reports.

5 Why is long-term growth and indirect impact not immediately visible?
There's often a disconnect in how marketing value is communicated and linked to company goals and metrics.

Marketing really does take time and the impact it makes often isn't trackable with software. You're dealing with humans, so this is logical. It also means that getting buy-in on your strategy is critical.

Tactics That Can Help You Get Buy-In but Won't Guarantee You Do

Remember how everything is made up? Getting buy-in is one of those areas where making stuff up can work in your favor. But before you do, it's helpful to know some common tactics that work. Get good at those, then start experimenting.

Be Curious

The first, most obvious thing you can do is be curious.

If you want your boss to see your point of view, then first do whatever you can to see theirs. And by see I mean *understand* without judgment. (Trust me, we know when you're judging, you're really bad at hiding it.)

This is hard, because to see it, you'll have to free yourself of a whole lot of assumptions and judgments you've made that you forgot are even there. I'm not saying you need to like what you see, but if you want leverage, the best advice I can give you is to stop thinking about right and wrong, so you are able to see the logic behind their actions and decisions. Now again, this logic may not be *logical* to you, but that's not the point. What you're looking for is the "why" driving their decisions, so you know how to make them feel *heard*, because that will position you better to get your way.

The "how" will vary by company and executive, but the "what" will reveal itself once you understand the invisible things driving their decisions:

- who they are accountable to

- who they are influenced by
- what motivates them (think ego-driven stuff)
- what demotivates them
- how they best receive information (i.e. timing, medium, format, tone)

Make Their Lives Easier

The best way to do that is to come up with a plan that makes their lives easier (or at least feels like it to them) and, at the very least, demonstrates reverence to a few key constraints they have to consider—money being the biggest one. To do that, they would appreciate two or three options with cost, timeline, and resource variables that wouldn't just work but are GOOD. Bonus if you can show that it accomplishes or contributes to more than one CURRENT objective, doesn't require social capital (bonus 2x if it earns them more social capital), shows simple results that don't require interpretation to show it worked, and doesn't require them to do anything or spend a ton of money.

> Your objective isn't to convince your boss that your strategy is correct; it's to convince your boss to let you do it.

The person you're trying to convince doesn't necessarily have to understand—or even buy in to—every aspect of your strategy to say yes. Especially when it comes to the CEO and CFO. Sometimes the less they know the better. When you think about getting buy-in from that perspective, the job to be done is often a lot simpler.

Tie It to Revenue

Nobody funds "visibility." If you can show a straight line from your strategy to revenue, then it's a cost that's eligible to be cut. Since straight lines don't do a good job of expressing the revenue impact of marketing, try working this into your argument:

Quantify the risk of doing nothing. What happens if they ignore your plan? Will the pipeline dry up? Will competitors eat your market share? People fear loss more than they crave gain—use that.

Call a Spade a Spade

When the CEO and CMO see "case study" in your content marketing plan, are they envisioning the same thing? Jeff Bull, former Head of DevRel at Cisco recommends you figure that out in the beginning:

> Think of it like creating a shared dictionary with your stakeholders. When someone says they want "more engaging content," ask them to describe what engagement means to them. When they request "better leads," have them define what makes a lead better. This practice might seem basic, but it's especially crucial in larger organizations where teams often operate with different unstated assumptions. The time you spend clarifying expectations upfront will save weeks of revisions and potential conflicts later.

Make sure you are both operating under the same understanding of EXACTLY what a spade is, what it's used for, etc., before you get too deep into execution. This is probably the most common challenge I ran into as a marketer and the majority of the work I do with my clients now: making sure we're on the same page... constantly!

SAMPLE EMAIL FRAMEWORK FOR INITIAL PITCH

Sometimes your first step is getting on the executive's calendar. Here's a framework for an email that has consistently high success rates:

Subject: Revenue Opportunity: **[Business Outcome]** Through Strategic Marketing Initiative

Hi [*Name*],

I've identified a specific opportunity to [*business outcome*] by addressing [*challenge/gap*] we're currently facing. Based on our analysis, this represents approximately [*quantified value*] in [*revenue/pipeline/cost savings*].

I'd appreciate 15 minutes to walk you through:

- the data behind this opportunity
- our recommended approach
- the expected business impact
- the resources required

Would [*specific date/time*] work for a brief discussion? I'll come prepared with a focused recommendation that requires minimal time investment from you.

Thank you,

[*Your Name*]

This template works because it:

- focuses immediately on business impact in the subject line
- opens with a specific opportunity rather than a marketing initiative
- quantifies potential value upfront
- respects the executive's time with a short, structured meeting request
- makes it clear you're bringing a recommendation, not just an idea

Be Objective

You will never get buy-in if you're too married to your idea.

Your ideas should be flexible (and so should you). When you prepare your pitch, critique your own ideas, and find the holes. The best ideas are malleable. They have multiple exits and paths forward. You're more likely to get approval if you can show that you've accounted for multiple outcomes and can thus reduce risk.

Remember: There is no single "Way" that God ordained as best.

The Power of Pilots

One of the most effective approaches for getting buy-in for new marketing initiatives is to start with small, controlled experiments that prove your concept before asking for larger investments. Pilots work because they:

- reduce perceived risk by limiting initial investment

- create tangible proof points executives can understand
- allow for refinement based on real-world feedback
- build credibility for your strategic thinking

Create Executive Champions

Every company has informal power structures alongside the formal org chart. Identifying and cultivating supporters within the executive team can dramatically increase your chances of securing buy-in. Make sure you build these relationships before you need them! With the right executive champion(s), your marketing initiatives gain credibility and an internal advocate who can help navigate potential resistance.

Executive Alignment: The Real Work of Marketing Leaders

The most important work you do as a content marketer is visible. The most important work you do as a content marketing leader is invisible and you'll rarely get acknowledged for it.

Your to-do list changes as your job becomes less about production and more about strategic alignment. It feels like you're doing work that doesn't matter because it's behind the scenes. The type of work you don't get credit for.

Much of your time will be spent in meetings establishing executive and cross-departmental alignment for your marketing initiatives.

Spend your time getting your executive team bought into your vision and the rest of the year will be easier for you. Success as a marketing leader isn't about executing successful campaigns—it's about building trust with the executive team, so you can do the campaigns in the first place.

Stop Doing the Work and Start Reporting on It

When leaders are executing, it's a sign they don't know how to lead.

Okay, harsh, but still: A lot of the times when leaders come to me stressed out, it's because they don't know how to lead, so they default to what's comfortable to them: doing.

And content marketers do tend to fall into this trap. Like, a lot of them. Probably most. Sorry, it's true.

But it's not entirely your fault. Basically, you spend all these years learning content marketing by executing and producing. You've learned the best practices and the tools. You've learned different processes and likely chosen, tweaked, and perfected a method that you now believe in like bacon: It's good. You've had to defend your ideas more than a few times to your boss, quantifying the value of your creative ideas. You've had, perhaps led, countless meetings, maybe even had a few direct reports.

So what do you do with all these skills? One big mistake people make is to use them to produce even more great work. Writing, editing, and content promotion skills can only take you so far. Instead, you need to use those skills to remove blockers for your team, advocate for the resources they need, communicate their wins, and help them succeed.

The Cold, Hard Truth

Once you nominally adopt an executive mindset, invest in relationship building with your CEO and others in the C-suite, as well as anyone at the company they really like, then you'll have up to a 50 percent chance of getting buy-in for your marketing strategy.

I know what you're thinking: A little snarky, eh?

Nope. It's just the way things are, and if you accept it without judging you'll create space in your brain for curiosity, which has way more potential to help you get what you want than complaining. Think of it like focusing your energy on you vs. focusing on them.

If you accept how it is now, you're in a much better position to change it... in your favor.

Then you need to create messaging that resonates with them by tailoring your story to the things they care about to show you understand and care about those things too. That means including certain details and leaving others out. And when they ask you questions and try to get into the details you know aren't helpful to them, you need to have sub-messaging prepared to redirect them to the shiny object you want them to focus on.

Every barrier is a creative constraint. It's a challenge to be more creative, clever, and experimental.

Maintaining Buy-in Companywide

Getting initial approval is just the first step. Maintaining support for your marketing strategy requires ongoing effort:

- set clear expectations
- establish realistic performance goals
- call out what could go wrong in advance
- remind, remind, remind: weekly, monthly, quarterly
- host in a public place and reference back to it in future updates to show consistency

The Write-up

Answer the question: How do you know if it's leading to business outcomes?

The CEO doesn't know what data they want, either. Which data to include and how much detail is too much is always a challenge.

They also don't know what a "good write-up" is either, even if they send you an example.

If it's not familiar, they're not going to like it, even if it's a good idea, so you have to really plan for that and get help from your executive sponsors.

If they read it at all, which is highly unlikely, your CEO is only going to skim the first page and determine quickly and flippantly, "yeah this looks good" or "ok this is good, a lot to talk about here, schedule a meeting with..." The latter means they don't like it for no particular reason or you caught them on a bad day and you're about to go through several unnecessary meetings during which your strategy will be picked apart and transformed into a grapefruit. Then when you return with the updated Grapefruit strategy, your C-suite will hate it and ask you why you thought the Grapefruit strategy made sense, and a few weeks later you'll be kicking off your original strategy halfway through the quarter and probably be on thin ice with the CEO (but they won't tell you).

Here's the thing you need to accept right now: You're going to spend way more time on this than they are going to know.

Stay Calm and Lead Meetings

Meetings are auditions for budding senior leaders. How you conduct yourself indicates to your boss the kind of leader you will be (or not). There are a few best practices if your goal is to be seen by leadership in a positive light:

- **Speak succinctly and slowly:** Speaking fast makes you look nervous. Saying more than is necessary to get the point across makes you look green. Take a deep breath, and exhale what you want to say. By the time you need to breathe in again, you should have made your point.

- **Ask questions:** The best leaders elevate above the fray by asking useful questions that help the team come up with an answer. If you want to demonstrate your leadership skills in meetings, but you aren't sure what to contribute, begin by asking a question.

- **Listen:** Listen to your boss, listen to the intern, listen to everyone. All great leaders are great listeners. You don't want to suck all the air out of the room by talking too much, so make sure you give everyone your full attention when it's their turn to speak.

- **Make meetings effortless:** Make meetings better by preparing. Make them more useful by taking notes, making sure everyone knows what to do next and following up on those items. The benefit to all this planning is that you have a flawless meeting where people go away feeling happy because they know the outcome, next steps, and what is expected of them.

Meetings are a great opportunity for junior employees to take on senior roles. No one loves running meetings, which makes them a perfect stage to take ownership and level up.

Don't Lose Your Cool, Even When Everyone Else Does

I've experienced some of the poorest behavior in my life at work. I've had a CEO call me a "chicken with my head cut off" in front of the entire company. Another CEO canceled a project during the kickoff meeting with no explanation, even after he'd approved and invested hundreds of human hours in it. I've seen executives shout unnecessarily, storm off, and generally waste employees' time because they were unprepared, didn't know how to lead meetings, or just plain didn't know how to lead.

Bad behavior at work shouldn't be an invitation to join the kindergarten class, it should be an example of what not to do. This happens in meetings all the time. An important meeting devolves into a bunch of people talking over one another, each insistent that their voice is heard. Leadership will definitely recognize the person in the room who asks a question that finally leads to a good discussion, or comes up with a solution that everyone can agree on.

Be that person even when it's tempting to join the fray.

Be Prepared to Negotiate

Expect to have your idea challenged. When you create an idea by reasoning from the facts rather than leaning on best practices or external data, you'll have stronger points to leverage in negotiation. **Negotiation tips:**

- listen more than you speak
- ask questions... and ask more follow-up questions
- take long pauses to think
- being forthcoming about what went wrong really helps build trust
- sharing what could go wrong in advance helps build trust

What has to happen for your goals to be realized?

Observe with the Objectivity of a Scientist

This is the one time when emotions of any kind will not serve you. If you can do this, you have a shot at getting some form of buy-in (this is an important point: You have to prepare your pitch knowing that negotiation will be involved).

Stop Talking About What You Deserve

Leaders SELL. They make the case for what they want by showing value in doing it for the person they need to convince.

Understand the mechanics. How the whole revenue cycle works. What the CEO is worried about. Talk to product and engineering about what concerning signals they see in app behavior. Talk to investors if you can. Your best chance of coming up with a smart strategy is to know as many of the pieces as possible and keep in touch with those folks as you're building to get their input—not necessarily on the strategy itself, but on things you're trying to validate.

Everything everyone does is made up and therefore subjective to their own motivations, circumstances, knowledge, etc. They are making up solutions to serve themselves and the situation they are in. You can do the same!

Find Out Who Is Judging

Who are your bosses accountable to? What are the expectations on them? Everyone has a boss. Executives have several. Find out:

- Who are they and how many?
- Why are they the authority (e.g. based on knowledge or position or both)?
- How much do they really know?
- What are they motivated by?
  - stakeholders
  - money
  - themselves
  - whatever it is they feel they have to prove

Getting What You Want Is a Decision

Have you ever played tug-of-war with a monkey? I have, and it's not as fun as you might think.

The story goes like this: I was taking a morning stroll with a friend in Bali (where I lived at the time) when a monkey snatched my friend's sweatshirt off her shoulders. To be fair (to the monkey, that is), we were in the Monkey Forest, and my friend, she'd been trying to lure this wild animal to her person so she could snap a cute selfie with it perched on her shoulders.

There I was standing opposite this creature, this monkey who had been sooooo adorable from far away but now held the fate of my friend's hoodie in his hand, and he was ready for a fight.

I felt helpless (though less helpless than my friend, who just cried): How do you recover stolen goods from a monkey?

I asked a park employee for help, but he wouldn't assist unless I gave him money, and I didn't have any. What I did have was an empty water bottle, which the park employee told me that I—personally without his help—could use to lure the monkey away from the sweatshirt.

And it worked! My cheap plastic Poland Springs bottle distracted the monkey, causing him to drop my friend's hoodie and lunge for the shiny thing in my hand.

Unfortunately, just as I thought I had cleared the shirt from the monkey's reach, he side-eyed like a boss, caught on to my plan, and grabbed a dangling sleeve before I could break the hoodie free from his grasp.

We were in a face-off, me tugging the hoodie one way and the monkey tugging the other (yep, this really happened and nope, this was not my finest moment). Again, I felt helpless—how was this going to end? What would become of my friend's precious hoodie?

Then something dawned on me: I'm bigger and stronger than this monkey.

So, I snatched the sweatshirt from his tiny hands and walked away.

The difference between helpless Tug-of-War-Devin and Victorious-Sweatshirt-Rescuer-Devin is simple: a decision. I stopped wanting the hoodie and decided I was going to have it.

Sure, I had the upper hand (I was bigger and stronger), but I was also facing an unknown foe, and I didn't know for certain that being bigger and stronger was an advantage. But instead of standing around worrying about the situation I was in, I took action and attempted to dictate the outcome. I didn't know if it was going to work; all I knew was that if I kept standing around fretting about what might happen, the monkey would end up with the sweatshirt anyway.

The thing is, life isn't always as dramatic as the movies. It's not about A Few Big Decisions That Change The Course Of Everything All Of A Sudden. It's actually a series of small choices that add up to your current circumstance, which is both a relief and a distress at the same time: You don't have to make so many Big Decisions, but you do need to make smaller ones on a regular basis. And if you want to be happy, then you have to decide in your own favor more often and take an active role in making it happen.

Crisis as Opportunity

Market shifts, competitor moves, and company challenges often create unique openings for new approaches. When the status quo is disrupted, executives become more receptive to fresh thinking.

During my time at Animalz, our opportunity came with the pandemic. As companies faced uncertainty, they slashed marketing budgets across the board—except for content. Content suddenly became the only marketing channel many companies could justify because it offered long-term value while requiring relatively modest investment compared to events, paid acquisition, and other channels that were suddenly ineffective.

This crisis opened executive minds to content approaches they'd previously dismissed. The temporary reduction in marketing options created space for deeper strategic conversations about content's role in the overall marketing mix.

As a marketing leader, you should be prepared to identify these moments of receptiveness:

- when competitors make significant strategic shifts
- during budget planning cycles

- after disappointing quarterly results
- following leadership changes
- during major market disruptions

These inflection points are when executives are most willing to consider new approaches. Having your strategy ready—with clear ties to business outcomes—positions you to capitalize on these moments of opportunity.

Conclusion: Leaders Don't Wait for Opportunity, They Create It

Getting buy-in for your marketing strategy is as much about politics and relationships as it is about the strategy itself. By focusing on creating common ground, establishing clear definitions of success, and adopting an executive mindset, you can transform the way your marketing initiatives are perceived and supported within your organization. Remember that the most important work you'll do as a marketing leader might be invisible, but it's what enables everything else to happen.

Takeaways:

- Clarify expectations and create a shared dictionary with stakeholders before beginning work.
- Focus on building trust with executives rather than convincing them your strategy is perfect.
- Learn to speak the language of business outcomes, not just marketing metrics.
- Use the Common Ground Framework to find areas of agreement and build from there.
- Adopt an executive mindset by understanding what drives their decisions.
- Make your ideas flexible and have alternatives ready for negotiation.
- As you move into leadership, stop doing the work and focus on removing blockers for your team.

- Use meetings as opportunities to demonstrate leadership skills.
- Maintain composure even when others don't.
- Help CEOs understand their role in marketing success: setting objectives, providing resources, and holding the team accountable.

No one is going to make you a leader. You have to lead yourself into a leadership role. Take the reins, create your own opportunity, and build the career that you deserve. If leadership isn't bought in, that's not just a them problem. It's also a you problem. So sell it like your budget depends on it—because it kind of does.

12

Building a Content Culture: Cross-Functional Collaboration

The second time I was fired, I was a mid-career marketer and decided to give freelancing a try.

My biggest worry when I embarked on this journey wasn't getting clients—that was just hitting the pavement-type stuff. The thing that had me worried: *Would my creativity stall working alone?*

Without the benefit of corporate constraints, a boss, and coworkers to collaborate with, would I still be able to come up with good ideas for my clients?

I shared this problem with my dad, and he had a different take. And, typical of my father, who's a huge music buff, he described it through the history of a song: "With a Little Help from My Friends."

He told me that the version of the song we all know today is actually an adaptation from the original written by Paul McCartney and Ringo Starr. That version was released in 1967 and two years later, Joe Cocker covered it live at Woodstock with some changes.

Most notably, he changed the lyrics from, "What would you *think* if I sang out *of* tune?" to "What would you *do* if I sang out *a* tune?" A change that even Ringo Starr himself adopted when he sang it. Later, Cocker also introduced a new musical element, an extended guitar portion performed by Jimmy Page. Now, when groups like Mumford and Sons and Tedeschi Trucks cover it, they mimic Cocker and Page's rendition rather than the original.

So the Beatles had an idea and shared it with the world. Then Cocker and Page heard it, added some tweaks, and voila. A good idea is transformed into a legendary piece of art. A form of distant collab-oration, a remote riff that turned just another song into a beloved piece of history.

Great story, *dad*. But what's your point?

The point, he said, is that collaboration, inspiration, creative ideas, they can come from anywhere. They can come from a book, a conversation with a stranger, a song. They don't have to come from the people sitting right next to you. "And," he said, "What if now the walls of your business are just further apart and there's more and different stuff housed between them?"

When you look at it that way, he said, don't you now have the ability to come up with even *more* ideas?

Making the Case for Content

Just as no piece of content marketing can exist in a vacuum, neither can your content marketing exist solely within the marketing team.

Without cross-functional collaboration, even the most brilliant content strategy will eventually collapse under the weight of competing priorities and misaligned expectations. Which makes it more than a nice-to-have—it's a necessity.

It's also unlikely that the suggestions I offer in this chapter will ever fully come together at your organization. That's ok! Leaders and teammates come and go, and when they do, things change both conveniently and inconveniently. My goal with this chapter is to give you options to help you get what you need from the folks on your team.

So, think of this chapter as a toolbox, not a desired future state. You only need collaboration and alignment to the extent that you can accomplish your objectives. You don't need folks to believe what you believe, you just need to make the case that it's in their best interest to collaborate. Some will be bought in from the start. Others will require some campaigning and perhaps even favor trading.

Your best chance at building a content "culture" that serves your objectives is to be objective about it yourself. Don't get too attached to other people's thoughts, attitudes, and opinions. You have something you want to accomplish, so keep your focus there. Remember: Building a content culture is a means to an end, not a moral imperative, so work on what you can control to get the outcomes you want.

Now, this next part you already know, but you also need me to say it, so feel free to just tear this section out and send it to your executive team then move on to the next section.

Why Building a Content Culture Matters

When the executive team is bought in on content as a working tool for growing the company, everything changes. Your marketing stops being perceived as a separate function that occasionally requests input from other departments and starts being understood as a core business process that everyone contributes to and benefits from—most of all, the business itself. This shift creates several strategic advantages:

1. Resilience During Leadership Changes

One of the most common killers of content marketing programs is leadership turnover. A new CMO arrives with different priorities, and suddenly the content strategy that took two years to build is scrapped overnight.

When content is embedded in your company culture, it becomes more resistant to these disruptions. Multiple departments have a stake in its success, protection, and continuation.

2. Higher-Quality, More Diverse Content

Content created in marketing isolation tends to lack the depth, specificity, and authenticity that comes from true subject matter expertise.

When engineers contribute to technical content, when customer support shapes troubleshooting guides, when sales teams inform competitive positioning—the result is richer, more accurate, more valuable content that genuinely helps your audience.

3. Built-in Distribution Networks

When content creation involves multiple departments, those departments become invested in its success. They share it with their networks, reference it in customer conversations, and use it in their daily work.

This creates organic distribution channels that extend far beyond your marketing email list or social media following. Your sales team become content advocates in prospect calls. Your customer success team share relevant pieces with clients facing specific challenges. Your engineers reference technical articles in developer forums and communities.

4. Increased Content ROI

Content created for multiple use cases delivers higher return on investment. A single piece of thoughtful, cross-functional content might:

- generate leads through SEO (marketing goal)
- address common objections in sales conversations (sales goal)
- help customers use features more effectively (customer success goal)
- showcase your technical innovation to potential recruits (HR goal)
- position your leadership team as industry experts (executive goal)

This multiplier effect transforms content from a marketing expense to a company-wide asset with diverse returns. But for this to work, you need to take ownership of communicating—and celebrating—these results internally.

5. Enhanced Brand Authenticity

When your content reflects the collective knowledge, experiences, and voices within your organization, it naturally becomes more authentic. This authenticity builds trust with your audience in ways that marketing-only content simply cannot.

The Reality Check: Why Cross-Functional Collaboration Often Fails

Despite these benefits, most B2B companies struggle to establish and maintain functional collaboration across departments. In my work with hundreds of B2B companies, I've consistently seen the same barriers:

Competing Priorities and Inertia

Every person and department has their own targets, deadlines, and metrics. Adding content contributions to already-full plates often feels like an imposition rather than an opportunity. When you're selling to folks in specialized fields or you need access to the C-suite for content, it can be difficult to hit your deadlines since those are often the ones with the least available bandwidth.

They may also be shy! I recall working with a cofounder for a blog post and he clammed up when I recorded on video. So, I offered to interview him in a conference room using my phone to record audio, and I kept it face down so he didn't feel like he was "on stage." It worked great; we talked for over an hour and I got everything I needed from him.

If I were in the same situation today, I might encourage him to record a voice note and send me the transcription. Perhaps provide a few specific questions to answer or provide a topical prompt. Whatever the barrier is, we have more tools available to get around.

Another common hangup I've experienced is experts believing they have nothing interesting to say or simply not feeling comfortable standing on a digital podium sharing their opinion. Founders, engineers, marketers—all brilliant people who had strong aversions to any kind of public personal brand content. The psychology behind this one varies, so I can't offer a one-size-fits-all solution other than:

- make a case that triggers their intrinsic motivations essential to accomplishing the one thing they really want;
- keep trying—sometimes they come around!

Lack of Structured Processes

Most companies lack clear processes for cross-departmental content collaboration. Without defined workflows for requesting input, managing reviews, scheduling subject matter expert (SME) interviews, and giving credit, collaboration becomes ad hoc and unsustainable.

Here's the thing: I've seen processes work and not work at companies large and small, and accounting for all the factors would take up the entire *Encyclopedia Britannica*. In my experience, process is super helpful in the early days of building a team, kind of a hinderance when you're in the small-medium growth phase, and crucial when you get medium-large and bigger. That part isn't really important.

What I can say is that honoring process for process's sake can also be a hinderance and lead to a deterioration of product quality, so make sure you're being flexible. Remember, you are trying to achieve an objective. Process helps and sometimes it's more helpful to bend the rules. Don't be too persnickety here.

Misaligned Incentives

This is the biggest thorn for marketers and sales teams in my experience and most likely you're nodding your head as you read this! I consulted for a growth marketing agency once where lack of alignment between marketing and sales was THE reason they weren't hitting their goals. Our account managers tried to flag with our POC, but she was junior and, it turned out, wasn't communicating our findings to the CMO. For months. Meanwhile, the sales team, who did have an experienced team lead, made a very convincing case to the CMO that marketing—and the agency—were doing a bad job.

The challenge for us: Since our POC refused to organize a meeting with their sales team and the CMO to sort it out, we were stuck. Given they had data that, to them, showed we were doing a bad job (ahem, this is why data isn't the truthteller some claim it is—it's often just fodder for good storytellers), I knew it was only a matter of time until we were fired.

My solution: I got the CEO of the agency to email the CMO, because they had a relationship already. I drafted the email for him, which essentially said that we were going to fire ourselves as their agency if she didn't get on the phone with us. It worked and the conversation we had with her was *uncomfortable*, but it worked. We got the big alignment meeting and she gave us a new POC who had more experience to help execute the campaign the way we suggested.

Here's my point: Sales teams are evaluated solely on meeting their quota, product teams on release deadlines, and support teams on ticket resolution times, so the way a lot of companies are run, there's little incentive for them to contribute to content efforts that don't directly impact their performance metrics.

Knowing that and accepting that as current reality, whether it's logical or not, will help you start thinking objectively about how to solve it. And yes, sometimes the answer will make you feel like the "bad guy." That junior POC we worked with? She got fired a few weeks later, even after we took the blame. It was obvious where the breakdown had occurred, and I knew going in that my approach to fixing the problem for the client would put our POC at risk. It's up to you to make the call on what you feel is right. I've settled on my own approach: Set people up for success but don't force them there. They may not like you, but they'll benefit more from falling on their face than you trying to drag them along with you.

Communication Breakdowns

Different departments often speak different "languages." Marketing terminology can sound like meaningless jargon to engineers. Technical specifications can be impenetrable to marketers. Without translation, these communication gaps prevent effective collaboration.

My advice: Say what you mean instead of leaning on jargon. If a word can be interpreted, use a different one or include your interpretation of it when you use the word.

"Accepting reality doesn't mean you have to abide by it."

And do try to understand the basics of the folks you're collaborating with. I worked with engineers, designers, and devs at every company I worked for, and I made an effort to remember what they taught me: Write Jira tickets the way they wanted, I even learned enough code to make some iframe thing one time that earned me an appreciative nod I'll always remember.

My point is: If you want folks to collaborate with *you*, then forget about process or what's considered "your job." Sticklers rarely get anything done.

The Fundamentals of Cross-Functional Content Collaboration

Creating a true content culture requires more than occasional requests for subject matter experts to review blog posts. It requires intentional bridge building that makes content creation valuable for everyone involved.

Here are a few approaches that have worked for me:

Start with Relationship Building

Before jumping into content workflows and processes, focus on building genuine relationships with key stakeholders across departments. This human foundation makes everything else possible.

QUESTIONS THAT BUILD RELATIONSHIPS

"I'm curious to learn more about your perspective on the criteria we use to qualify leads at this stage of the journey. I know we've butted heads on this before, so I'm asking you one-to-one because nothing ever gets solved in meetings and honestly, if I can understand you better, I think we can overcome the blocker more effectively on our own."

"What do you hate the most about our marketing?"

"What do you think marketing should start doing? Have you shared ideas in the past that got shot down? What are they?"

"What do I need to know about x person to help me approach/work with them without annoying them? Are there specific things I can do to demonstrate I'm serious about collaborating with them?"

"What do I need to know about you to stay on your good side? The way I see it, I can't achieve x or y without you/your support, so as much as I'd like to say this is purely altruistic, it's partly selfish, too. But that also means I'm incentivized to build a strong relationship with you, so tell me what it takes."

These questions may seem direct, even uncomfortably so, but they cut through the corporate niceties that often prevent real collaboration. They signal that you're interested in genuine partnership rather than transactional interactions.

Find Common Ground

As Suneet Bhatt, my former boss, the CMO from Help Scout, explains:

> I think the hardest thing and the most important thing you can do in any context is to think politically and listen to everybody. When you are trying to build something that requires collaboration across departments, you look for the positive areas of agreement. You can't be critical. You can't find the areas of difference. You have to find the areas of hope and common ground. Then you have to protect and nurture the hell out of those areas of common ground. And then you will start to see cross-team collaboration bloom.

In practice, this means identifying the shared goals that content can help achieve. Things like:

- sales teams want to close more deals
- product teams want customers to understand and use features
- support teams want to reduce repetitive tickets
- HR wants to attract talented candidates
- executives want to raise the company's profile and valuation

Content can serve all these goals when approached strategically. Your job is to make those connections explicit.

At Help Scout, Suneet found his common ground in customer-centricity:

> At Help Scout, I was able to get everybody to align around the customer. And the only decisions that worked were when I labeled things "customer." Customer success worked, customer onboarding worked, customer community. Everything we pitched, as long as we put it in service to the customer, we could get stuff done. And then over time, we were able to start drawing straight lines from content to new customers.

Finding this unifying principle—whether it's customer focus, industry leadership, technical excellence, or another shared value—gives everyone a reason to invest in content collaboration.

Align Incentives and Recognition

For cross-functional collaboration to work, it must align with how people are evaluated and rewarded. This alignment of incentives transformed content from "extra work" to "valued contribution."

Create Feedback Loops

True collaboration is a two-way street. It's not just about getting input from other departments—it's about showing them how that input creates value. Establish regular reporting mechanisms that show the impact of collaborative content:

- monthly emails to contributors showing how their content performed
- quarterly reviews with department heads highlighting cross-functional wins
- dashboards tracking how content is supporting various departmental goals
- recognition in all-hands meetings for successful collaborations

These feedback loops demonstrate that collaboration is worthwhile, creating motivation for continued participation.

SPREADING JOY AS A MARKETING METRIC
Justine Jordan, *Head of Strategy and Community*

As a self-funded "anti-venture studio," Wildbit, maker of the popular email delivery service Postmark (acquired by ActiveCampaign in 2022), didn't face the same pressures for immediate results that VC-backed companies do. This gave us the freedom to prioritize team fulfillment and experiment with creative approaches that might take longer to show results.

During one of our experimentation weeks when team members could build whatever they wanted in one week, a delightful comic called "The Postmark Express" was born.

Derek, our product designer, and Jordan, who works in customer success, teamed up to create a prototype of a web comic about email deliverability—a topic that's technically complex, often dry, but critically important to our customers.

The prototype sat on the shelf for a couple of quarters, but we kept talking about revisiting it. As we were building our marketing team, we were thinking about how to optimize for team fulfillment and help people explore their careers without leaving Wildbit. That's when we created the concept of "marketing rotations," where people could spend a quarter working with another team.

Derek and Jordan joined the marketing team for Q3 to work on the comic. Derek had been using his Fridays to learn illustration and explore artistic endeavors. Jordan used his "success days"—the one day per week

FIGURE 12.1 Postmark Express

that customer support team members get to work on other projects—to develop the script with help from other team members.

ALL ABOARD THE POSTMARK EXPRESS

"The Postmark Express" became a western-themed comic that helped people who didn't understand email deliverability learn about it in a fun way, while also giving email professionals something they can share with others who don't understand what they do.

It follows a character named Jordan (based on our actual team member) who sends an email to his friend Lucy. The email turns into an adventure when Jordan, represented as a dog, gets sucked into the internet and meets a cast of characters who help him understand how his email gets delivered.

SPREADING JOY AS A METRIC

As the head of marketing, I needed to think about how to market this comic in a way that honored its creativity and didn't feel like a marketing gimmick.

We realized that the comic had the potential to bring joy to multiple audiences: People unfamiliar with email deliverability would enjoy the story itself, email professionals would appreciate seeing their work represented, and content marketers might be inspired by our approach.

So we decided to set joy as our KPI. Could we optimize for joy? Could we even measure it?

We supported this primary goal with some traditional marketing metrics: getting into the top 10 on Product Hunt (so we'd be featured in their email newsletter), building an email list with people interested in the comic, and setting page view goals.

IMPACT AND LESSONS LEARNED

This kind of marketing is hard to measure directly. You can't look in a dashboard and see the number of heart emojis you got on Twitter. But it builds brand affinity, trust, and loyalty—things that translate to business health metrics like net dollar retention, reduced churn, and word-of-mouth referrals.

When we asked new Postmark customers why they chose us, about 15 percent said they were referred from somewhere else, and 13 percent said they'd used Postmark before at another company. Traditional attribution methods wouldn't capture these sources.

In business, we often focus too much on direct response and attribution. But sometimes the most valuable marketing creates experiences and relationships that can't be immediately measured—yet lead to devoted customers and authentic growth over time.

Department-by-Department Collaboration Frameworks

Each department has different priorities, expertise, and potential contributions to your content strategy. Here are some ways to establish consistent collaboration. Depending on the tools you have at your company, there are multiple opportunities to automate aspects of this process. Also, make sure to include your SEO person or team from the beginning because they will likely have ways to make some of these initiatives more impactful.

Sales Collaboration Framework

Sales teams have invaluable insights about customer objections, competitive positioning, and what messaging resonates in real-world conversations. They're also potential power users of your content in sales enablement contexts.

SALES COLLABORATION OPPORTUNITIES

1 Objection-based content:
   o have sales teams document common objections encountered in calls
   o create content that specifically addresses these objections
   o package this content for sales to use in follow-up emails
2 Competitive intelligence:
   o gather sales team insights on competitor messaging and positioning
   o create comparison content that highlights your differentiators
   o update this content regularly based on competitive shifts
3 Deal acceleration content:
   o identify common sticking points in the sales process
   o create content targeted at specific decision-maker personas
   o track how this content impacts deal velocity
4 Sales enablement materials:
   o transform marketing content into sales-ready formats

- o create customizable templates sales can personalize
- o build a searchable library of sales-ready content snippets

Product Collaboration Framework

Product teams bring deep technical knowledge and understanding of your solution's capabilities. They're essential for creating accurate, forward-looking content that positions your product effectively.

PRODUCT COLLABORATION OPPORTUNITIES

- Feature education content:
  - o develop in-depth explanations of complex features
  - o create use-case examples showing feature applications
  - o build comparison content showing your approach vs. alternatives
- Product roadmap content:
  - o create forward-looking thought leadership about your vision
  - o develop "coming soon" teasers that build anticipation
  - o document the thinking behind product decisions
- Technical deep dives:
  - o showcase your technical innovation and approach
  - o create content that demonstrates thought leadership
  - o build credibility with technical decision-makers
- User onboarding content:
  - o develop resources that help new users succeed
  - o create progressive learning paths for different user types
  - o build feature discovery content for existing users

Customer Success/Support Collaboration Framework

Customer-facing teams understand user challenges, questions, and success patterns better than anyone else in your organization. They're goldmines of practical, authentic content ideas.

CUSTOMER TEAM COLLABORATION OPPORTUNITIES

- Frequently asked questions:
  - transform common support questions into searchable content
  - create troubleshooting guides based on support tickets
  - develop self-service resources that reduce support volume
- Success stories:
  - identify customers achieving remarkable results
  - document their implementation approaches
  - create case studies and testimonials
- Usage optimization content:
  - develop advanced tutorials for power users
  - create content showing unexpected use-cases
  - build resources that help customers get more value
- Community content:
  - create resources that facilitate customer-to-customer help
  - develop moderation guidelines and conversation starters
  - highlight customer expertise through collaborative content

One of the most effective content collaboration systems I've seen came from a B2B software company whose support team maintained a "content gap" document. Support agents would add customer questions that didn't have good existing resources, along with the number of times they'd encountered that question. The content team then prioritized new content based on this real-world frequency data. Within six months, they reduced support tickets by 23 percent while increasing customer satisfaction scores.

Executive Collaboration Framework

Leadership team members bring strategic perspective, industry connections, and authority to your content. Their involvement can elevate content from informational to influential.

- Thought leadership:
  - develop signature perspectives on industry trends
  - create forward-looking content about market evolution
  - build executive brands that enhance company credibility
- Strategic narrative:
  - articulate company vision and differentiation
  - connect product strategy to market needs
  - position the company in the competitive landscape
- Industry commentary:
  - create timely responses to market events
  - develop perspectives on industry challenges
  - build a reputation for insight and foresight
- Community leadership:
  - represent the company in industry conversations
  - create content that builds community around shared values
  - position executives as accessible, authentic leaders

Engineering/Technical Team Collaboration Framework

Technical teams have the deep subject matter expertise in your organization, yet their insights rarely make it into your content without intentional collaboration.

TECHNICAL COLLABORATION OPPORTUNITIES

- Technical credibility content:
  - explain your technical approach and innovation
  - compare methodologies and architectural decisions
  - develop content that showcases technical excellence
- Developer education:
  - create resources that help technical users implement
  - develop tutorials, guides, and documentation

- build community around technical implementation
- Industry leadership:
  - share insights about technology trends and evolution
  - develop perspectives on technical challenges
  - build credibility in technical communities
- Technical case studies:
  - document complex implementation approaches
  - showcase creative technical solutions
  - demonstrate real-world impact of technical decisions

Making Content Collaboration Easier at Your Company

Now that we've explored the why and how of content collaboration, here are some ways you can implement. There's a lot here on purpose. I don't recommend you DO all of this. But knowing that every company is different, I wanted to include a bunch of ideas that you can combine to suit whatever your circumstances are.

Process and Resource Infrastructure

The goal is removing friction from the collaboration process. The easier you make it for non-marketing team members to contribute, the more likely they are to participate.

- **Content request system:** Simple forms or templates for anyone to suggest content ideas.
- **Subject matter expert (SME) database:** Directory of internal experts by topic area.
- **Content calendar:** Visible planning tool showing upcoming collaborations.
- **Asset library:** Organized repository of all published content.
- **Collaboration platforms:** Shared workspaces for content development.
- **Recognition system:** Process for crediting contributors.

Role and Responsibility Definitions

Clearly define how different departments and individuals contribute to content creation then document these roles in simple, clear language that sets expectations without creating bureaucracy.

- **Content owners:** Responsible for overall strategy and execution.
- **Subject matter experts:** Provide specialized knowledge and insights.
- **Reviewers:** Ensure accuracy and alignment with objectives.
- **Amplifiers:** Share and distribute content through their channels.
- **Executive sponsors:** Advocate for content initiatives at leadership level.

Motivational Systems

Build mechanisms that make content collaboration rewarding for everyone involved. Remember that different individuals are motivated by different rewards. Some value public recognition, others professional development, others visible business impact. Design your motivational systems to accommodate these differences.

- **Recognition programs:** Public acknowledgment of contributions.
- **Performance integration:** Including content contributions in reviews.
- **Career development:** Positioning content as a skill-building opportunity.
- **Impact reporting:** Showing how content influences business results.
- **Collaborative goal-setting:** Creating shared content objectives.

Continuous Improvement Processes

Create feedback loops that constantly enhance your collaborative content system:

- **Regular retrospectives:** Review what's working and what isn't.
- **Contributor surveys:** Gather feedback from participants.
- **Performance analysis:** Track which collaborative content performs best.

- **Process iterations:** Regularly update and improve your systems.
- **Success story sharing:** Highlight examples of effective collaboration.

No collaborative system is perfect from the start. These improvement processes help your content culture evolve and strengthen over time.

ESTABLISHING WHAT *GOOD* LOOKS LIKE

Jeff Bull, *Head of Developer Community, Orkas, previously at Cisco*

If you're going to embark on this big project—standing up an entire org within the company, for example—you can't possibly align with your stakeholders' expectations or goals if you don't know what those underlying criteria are.

I took a master class a few years ago with Tessa Kriesel, the former head of DevRel (Developer Relations) at Snap (Snapchat), on how to start your own DevRel organization. She suggested setting up meetings with all the stakeholders that you're going to support or interface with all the way up to senior executives and ask them things like:

- What do you think DevRel is?
- What does success look like to you?
- What do you expect?
- What are you looking for exactly when you say you want X thing?

What you're essentially asking is: "If I do all these things, are you going to say, 'That's not what I wanted you to do'"?

The same concept applies to marketing. If you create a case study the way *you* think is best and it doesn't match what your stakeholder(s) imagined, perception essentially becomes reality at that point.

If they don't recognize it as good, then it's not good.

The solution is deceptively simple: Schedule conversations with every stakeholder who will evaluate or sign off on your work, from your immediate supervisor to senior executives. Make sure that you understand what the tolerances for different types of things are at the company you work for. Ask them what their processes are, who should be approving stuff, who should you be going to talk to?

Particularly when you're working at a big corporation that has tons of layers, you cannot assume anything.

Overcoming Common Challenges

Even with the best systems in place, building a cross-functional content culture isn't always smooth sailing. Here are strategies for addressing common challenges:

Challenge: "We're Too Busy"

The most common objection to content collaboration is lack of time. Combat this by:

- **Timeboxing:** Strictly limit the time commitment required (e.g., 30-minute interviews).
- **Batching:** Group similar content activities to increase efficiency.
- **Preparation:** Do your homework before involving busy team members.
- **Alternative formats:** Use voice notes or quick video captures instead of written input.
- **Administrative support:** Handle scheduling and follow-up to minimize burden

Remember that brief, focused collaboration is better than comprehensive collaboration that never happens.

Challenge: Inconsistent Executive Support

If leadership enthusiasm for content collaboration waxes and wanes:

- **Tie to objectives:** Explicitly connect content to executive priorities.
- **Quick wins:** Demonstrate early success with minimal investment.
- **Competitive insight:** Show what competitors are achieving with collaborative content.

- **External validation:** Share industry recognition and customer feedback.
- **Clear ROI:** Provide tangible measurement of collaborative content impact.

The key is making content collaboration a strategic advantage, not a nice-to-have initiative.

Challenge: Departmental Silos

When departments resist collaboration due to entrenched silos:

- **Start small:** Begin with one receptive department to demonstrate success.
- **Find champions:** Identify and support collaboration advocates in each area.
- **Executive mandate:** Secure leadership direction on collaboration importance.
- **Shared metrics:** Create goals that require cross-functional cooperation.
- **Process integration:** Embed content collaboration in existing workflows.

Remember Suneet's advice about starting with common ground and nurturing areas of agreement. Build from points of connection rather than trying to force full-scale collaboration immediately.

Building Content Culture for the Long Term

Cross-functional content collaboration isn't a one-time initiative; it's an ongoing cultural evolution. Here are two major ways to ensure your content culture thrives long-term:

Make Content Collaboration Part of Onboarding

Introduce new employees to your collaborative content approach from day one:

- include content culture in organizational orientation

- highlight collaboration opportunities within each role
- showcase successful examples of cross-functional content
- connect new hires with content champions in their department

When content collaboration is presented as "how we work" rather than "a new initiative," it becomes part of your organizational DNA.

Develop Content Leaders Throughout the Organization

Identify and nurture content champions across departments:

- provide additional training and resources to interested individuals
- create "content ambassador" roles with specific responsibilities
- give these champions visibility and recognition
- involve them in strategic content planning
- support their content skill development

These distributed leaders extend your content culture's reach far beyond what the marketing team could achieve alone.

Conclusion: From Content Program to Content Culture

Throughout this book, we've explored strategies for creating high-impact growth strategy and content that drives business objectives. But ultimately, the difference between companies that occasionally produce good content and those that consistently build audience relationships through content is culture.

When content becomes cultural:

- it transcends marketing department boundaries
- it reflects authentic, diverse organizational expertise
- it serves multiple business objectives simultaneously
- it creates compounding value over time
- it becomes resistant to leadership or market changes

Building this culture isn't easy or quick. It requires intentional relationship building, thoughtful process design, and consistent commitment to collaboration. But the results—deeper customer connections, more efficient content production, and sustainable competitive advantage—make it one of the most valuable investments your organization can make.

> *"The most valuable marketing often creates experiences and relationships that can't be immediately measured—yet lead to devoted customers and authentic growth over time."*
>
> Justine Jordan

As I've seen throughout my career with companies of all sizes, the organizations that thrive aren't the ones with the biggest content budgets or the most sophisticated martech stacks. They're the ones that have successfully embedded content creation and distribution throughout their organizational DNA.

Remember how everything is made up? This is one of the places where that reality can work in your favor, if you take the opportunity.

This perspective applies not just to CEOs, but to every cross-functional relationship that supports your content culture. When you understand the driving motivations of sales, product, customer support, and other departments, you create the foundation for genuine collaboration rather than mandatory compliance.

Building a content culture isn't a one-time initiative. It's a continuous process of deepening relationships, refining processes, and expanding ownership. Start small, celebrate wins, learn from setbacks, and keep building. The competitive advantage it creates—authentic content that genuinely reflects your organization's collective expertise—can't be quickly replicated by competitors.

In the end, the most successful content marketers aren't necessarily the best writers or the most creative campaign designers. They're the ones who can weave content creation into the fabric of their organizations, transforming marketing from a department activity to a company-wide capability.

That transformation doesn't happen overnight, but with the principles and frameworks in this chapter, you have the foundation to start building your own cross-functional content culture—one that will survive leadership changes, market shifts, and technological disruptions. Because when content becomes cultural, it becomes sustainable. And in today's rapidly changing B2B landscape, that sustainability might be your most valuable marketing asset of all.

13

What Happens When It Doesn't Go to Plan?

Just because you get called to a fight doesn't mean you have to go.

MY MOM

Financial fraud has been a surprising theme in my career.

By accident, of course, and never invited, but it keeps showing up. So, I wasn't concerned when the COO of a company my client worked with accused me of it on a call.

Let me back up.

I was consulting for a growth marketing agency, helping the CEO with their business strategy and operations to prepare them to achieve more ambitious growth goals.

Among the company's many challenges, the service delivery team had been understaffed for months and their core service product was being mismanaged by the department head. By the time I arrived, many customers were unhappy and several projects were off course. The company had already experienced significant staff turnover in the previous year, so telling a portion of already upset customers that their account manager was going to change again—even though it benefitted them—didn't exactly give them confidence. Fair!

So, when I spoke with the VP of Marketing at Acme, Inc. for the first time, I was not surprised that she was really frustrated. She said progress had stalled due to all the turnover, and we were a whole quarter behind on the work we promised them. But that wasn't all. After reviewing their account, we found even more errors we'd made:

- not properly documenting completed work
- not sharing completed deliverables with the client
- marking work as complete when it wasn't
- lacking proper project management
- not checking in to make sure the original scope reflected their business's changing needs

And because the work we were doing was incredibly complex, not only was project management and execution deeply important, so was communication, and we'd done a poor job of that, too.

Not only were things not "going to plan," the entire project had gone off the rails.

To try to make things right, I collaborated with the growth agency's SVP of Client Services to account for our mistakes, dramatically reduce their fees and catch up on the work. Though the VP at Acme was initially on board and we got back to work, she continued to ask for more and more concessions. Many of these new requests were for work we had already delivered and they had accepted without issue.

Typical negotiation tactic—get as much as you can—and we'd really messed up, so I budged a little more, but let her know I'd be capping concessions there. We'd more than accounted for our mistakes with money and a new scope of work.

That's when the VP escalated to her COO. Again, typical. Using hierarchy to your advantage in negotiations is normal. Most likely, they'd been working on this together the entire time, choosing to keep the COO out of discussions until they hit a block and needed to escalate.

As soon as our SVP of Client Services and I got on the phone with Acme's VP of Marketing and COO, I saw the play. The COO played "aggressively angry" cop and the VP played Swiss negotiator—not exactly taking sides, but you knew who she was supporting.

The COO immediately shot off accusations, claiming we owed them an additional $100,000 on top of the work we were already doing at a drastically discounted rate, elegantly transitioning to his crescendo.

"This is financial fraud! I mean, there's no other way to see it. This is financial fraud!"

He played the part well. I was impressed. He seemed really mad! Younger me would have been terrified on that call, but today me knew he was playing a part to get what he wanted. And in making his move, I knew exactly what my next play would be.

"No, this is not financial fraud," I scoffed, calling his bluff. He continued yelling, I held my ground, and when he ran out of energy we agreed to wrap up the remaining work in three months.

We didn't exactly solve the problem. Acme, Inc. continued to ask for more work and concessions as we wrapped up. And they made sure those three months were painful, taking jabs at our team whenever they could. It was an unhappy situation until the end and pretty much nothing went right, no matter how hard the team tried.

This is also not the whole story. If I included all the details, you'd see a total calamity with long tentacles indicating fundamental issues on both sides that led to a conflict-ridden, money and reputation-losing situation that, at the point where I came in, was never going to have a fairytale ending.

And while this is a more extreme example, it is something that comes up time and time again—and why younger me would have been caught off guard by the whole thing, but older me now knows better. It's something I assume in every situation so that nothing ever surprises me anymore. And that is: *"It" never goes to plan.*

"It" Never Goes to Plan

The point of a plan is merely to get moving. After that, a whole bunch of things you have and have not accounted for will occur, requiring you to adapt the plan along the way. And since your biggest challenge will usually be getting approval for it in the first place, I recommend scoping enough of a plan that you know will get approval by your stakeholders, then just get started on anything at all as soon as possible.

Approximately two weeks into the project, expect the entire company, including your team, to forget every single thing they agreed on, including the fact that there is a project happening in the first place, despite you reminding them daily in Slack, reporting on it once a week and having multiple 1:1s with stakeholders in the meantime.

At some point, one of the marketers on your own team is going to complain to someone with influence that they "don't know what's going on" and it's going to get to your boss and they're going to believe whoever said it, and you're going to have to convince your boss that the project is still on track.

PRO TIP

For reasons I honestly don't know, it's tough to convince your boss that the project never actually went off track and it won't do you any good to try. Confoundingly, the more evidence you provide only makes you look worse to your boss. When this happens, I recommend simply showing how you've "solved" the fake problem and gotten things "back on track." Reality typically isn't worth the effort here—though it's time to have a chat with your direct report.

Keep your eye on the outcome. Rarely, if ever, will your plan come to complete fruition—and it doesn't matter. The plan was a means to the outcome you want. Don't forget that along the way by getting precious about the integrity of your plan. Your goal is fewest actions for greatest possible impact. And, like it or not, sometimes achieving that involves accepting ideas from people you don't like or acquiescing on superficial things that, if you really think about it, aren't that important anyway (I'm looking at you, Oxford comma!).

Most important, dear marketers, is that you develop the mental agility to manage with the focus and calm of a researcher when things inevitably don't go to plan. If you do, you will have the best chance of extracting some kind of benefit for you (as well as the company, when it's convenient).

Why It Doesn't Go to Plan

If you pack too many activities in your content strategy without a realistic, logical execution plan that accounts for your existing resources and constraints plus additional accommodation for unpredictable yet inevitable "sideways" events, will anyone see it?

NO. The answer is no. But you know that already. The things that really go wrong don't typically involve logic. They involve ego, internal politics, conflicting motivations, and input from executives who have strong opinions about marketing but have never done it before.

Your real objective, the strategy beneath your visible strategy, is to overcome the issues that block you from executing your plan. You're not trying to win an acknowledgment campaign. You're trying to get what you want, so stay focused on the problems you can solve.

To do that, you need some intel.

What's Going On with Your CEO?

To help you navigate around your CEO and C-suite to get your way more often, I'm going to share some of the circumstances they are working with that might be in part, if not entirely, invisible. None of what I share is intended to convince you that CEOs are worse off than you. They're not. In fact, comparing CEOs with most other roles at the company is unhelpful in the first place. A tomato may be a fruit, but no one ever puts it in a fruit salad.

The picture I'm going to paint is basic for the purpose of being useful. As in, I won't be describing world peace here. Instead, this picture, for me at least, is how I make my first principal understanding of CEOs, so that I can interact with them more productively. This is based on my experience as well as the many CEOs I know and have worked with, but it's not the whole story, so take from it what you like and leave the rest. In the end, your success depends more on what you *do* with knowledge than the amount of knowledge you have.

Pulling Back the Curtain

Your CEO is responsible first and foremost for the health of the company. Without the company, none of you would have a job there, so this is actually good and fine and correct. There are other types of corporate structures that work—Defector Media comes to mind—so if you don't like this structure, go work at a different type of company. But in all likelihood, you have a CEO to answer to. And that's ok. You just have to learn the wheel before you can create a different type of thing that moves objects forward with less brute human force. No matter what you believe you know from reading, your plan isn't going to work if you don't understand a system in practice.

The CEO has a boss, too—several, actually. So the next time you think they don't understand the reality that you're a Director of Content Marketing who has to get approval from the adjacent Product Marketing team, plus the VP of Marketing and occasionally the Head of Product's mom, trust me: Your CEO gets it. They, too, are being pulled in many different simultaneous directions all of which end with several people—if not all—being varying levels of unhappy with them.

Again, I'm not suggesting you feel bad for CEOs—you shouldn't, because they chose the job and that's part of it and they get paid the most to do it. What I am recommending is that you embrace this common ground with your CEO, even if it's only in your mind, so you can come up with more effective strategies to get your way.

Here's a non-exhaustive list of who a CEO is responsible to:

THE MONEY PEOPLE

Whoever gave them money to run the business: a bank loan, VC investment, angel investment, money they borrowed from their mom. To get that money, they had to make a business plan, which obviously includes how they will make and spend money and grow. This business must convince the money people that it could logically "work." And to the money people, "work" generally means it achieves one of the following:

- pay back the money they lent you on a schedule and cadence, typically with interest;

- make them *more* money than they invested in your company, but worst-case scenario, at least the amount they originally invested.

Well, sort of. This is basically so oversimplified that it's barely accurate. But for the sake of staying on course and having to become an armchair financial expert, let's just go with the simple version so I can get to the point.

For investors, the projections tend to be the most convincing because that's where the potential for Big Money Returns lies. It is also the cause of things like "growth at all costs" but that's a different book.

If you don't like how this works, 1) I don't blame you, 2) there are lots of small businesses that are bootstrapped or get loans that accommodate for growth styles that might be more appealing. The latter may not immediately provide a comparable salary to a larger company or mid-late-stage VC-backed startup, but you'll have more control over your own fate, both from a financial and equilibrium perspective. In this case, think of yourself as an investor and negotiate the terms that serve your big life goals, too.

THE TEAM

Here is what a team looks like from the CEO's point of view:

- the C-suite as a whole;
- each individual "C" within the C-suite;
- heads of any other departments in your company;
- the whole team as an organism with its collective mindset, impressions, etc.;
- each department's personality, desires, frustrations (which include discontent with other departments);
- small groups within departments, for example content marketing;
- loud individuals in the company who hate everything about the company but don't leave because they are a "victim" and it's all the company's fault (for some reason);
- individuals who don't say anything but are unhappy for specific reasons that are valid, perhaps solvable, definitely explainable, but

they aren't clear on what they want for themselves and, for right now, the cost-benefit of change just isn't there for them;

- individuals who believe the company should offer a perk or benefit that they believe is "cheap" (without doing math), "easy to implement" (probably not), and "every other company offers it."

CUSTOMERS

This includes:

- your customers who are happy;
- customers who are unhappy;
- customers who will be unhappy soon if you don't add this feature that no one in the company is excited about, least of all your engineering team;
- churned customers who hate the product;
- churned customers who leave quietly;
- anyone in the market who could be a customer now or in the future;
- someone your board member introduced you to;
- the 25 people a week who email you directly who could be a customer now or in the future;
- the 105 people who aren't potential that email you every week wanting something from you.

THE MARKET

Competitors, the media, their neighbors, their former colleagues, industry peers. All the people who exist in and around the ecosystem of the business. Though *the market* does also have technical meaning, in this context I'm referring to both tangible competitive factors as well as public perception since we're all only human, so this definitely always plays a part in a CEO's decisions (often on the larger side—it is what it is and until you're in the seat, it is to your strategic benefit that you stop judging it).

Then of course there's your vendors, partners, and some guy you have to talk to because he's friends with the CEO of your biggest customer's daughter, and it would really mean a lot to him.

On top of all this, the CEO has to consider whether the thing they are agreeing to is scalable. Can I sustain these benefits when we're 500, 1,000 people (if the plan is to get that big)? On the flip side, for small companies, and I experienced this myself, there are many things you want to give your team, build for your customers etc. right away, but you can't because you don't have the money and/or doing so would break your business model such that you will go out of business, so not only will you not provide the thing but also your team will be mad they don't have jobs and customers will be mad your product is gone.

Basically, there's hardly a decision the CEO makes that's simple in any way, which means a lot of your conspiracy theories are inaccurate. Then again, there are also a lot of corrupt leaders, so you're also sometimes right. What I'm trying to say—inelegantly—is that not all CEOs are jerks, and those who are tend to be bigger jerks than you imagine in ways you'll never even see.

Here's an example from Animalz to illustrate:

> I remember a time when a small group of folks on the team wanted the company to expand our benefits coverage to include children. So I asked my VP of People Ops to prepare a report summarizing the options and associated costs available.
>
> It turns out, providing additional benefits to folks with children was so expensive that we basically wouldn't earn a profit, which meant no bonuses for anyone, no money for stuff any other team member wanted (which was something like 80 percent of the company). What made it even more complicated was that we worked with folks in the United States and overseas and adding this benefit would only apply to the US folks with families. The math wasn't mathing.
>
> I told the team we couldn't add these benefits but did not share the precise reason why. From my point of view, going into detail about my decision would have inadvertently divided the team into factions of families, non-families, US team, non-US team. That could have caused even more conflict and lack of productivity among the team.

This is where it was my job as CEO to take the hit. Making me the person to blame was not only accurate (I did make the call) but it also ensured the team remained united, which was more important than them approving of my decision.

Now, given that the team was accustomed to my transparent leadership style, this did not go over well. Folks were upset and it kept coming up. It started to take up an inordinate amount of time across management and leadership and became a kind of sign to many folks that leadership could not be trusted.

I had to do something about it; though the same problem remained, the factual story was still divisive. So I tried another way.

Since we were transparent with the team about our finances at a business level, I decided to use our Profit and Loss (P&L) to explain the situation, but used dummy numbers (using the real ones would have been bad for other reasons). In so doing, I could provide more detail into how I made financial decisions and evaluated the impact they would have on the whole company.

The result was positive and predictable.

The majority of the team who were happy remained happy.

The ~10 percent of the team living in the United States who had families understood (for the most part) and some were even grateful for the explanation.

The ~20 percent of the team who had families and lived overseas didn't need explanation in the first place and were fine.

The less than 1 percent of the team who hated everything all the time, still did and some went to Glassdoor and called me a monster.

If you're working with logical, reasonable people, this won't be an issue. They may not say yes, but it'll make sense and they'll ensure you understand. If you're working with illogical people, keep your eye on the ball—the ball being wherever is *next* on your list. And remember, don't stay too long if it's not working out.

Agitation and discomfort, while occasionally signs of personal growth, are most often exactly what they seem: a normal reaction to toxicity levels that are unnatural for your absolutely strong enough already spirit to handle. But you're not off the hook, because the way out is all on you.

You don't deserve better if you don't choose it.

Creating a Plan B

Here's the secret no one tells you: In almost every situation at work, your biggest roadblock isn't a person or circumstance. It's ego and emotion. Every physical person standing in your way has their own agenda, and that agenda is based on their emotions and their ego. The faster you learn to decode *what's behind the scenes* of their objections, the faster you can get back to doing great work.

It's not enough to be right. Even the cleverest strategies get rejected almost entirely due to stakeholders' preexisting beliefs, knowledge, and experience being led by their ego- and emotion-based agenda. This is true and if you ever find an executive who agrees with this, go work for them immediately.

For everyone else—aka the vast majority of us—there are three ways emotion and ego will team up and challenge you.

I'm Helping!

Your CEO has an idea they want you to implement *right now*, even though it has nothing to do with your current strategy and investing in it will put your goals (which support their objectives) at risk.

Instead of trying to prove won't work, ask them to do the math on what it will cost them to change their mind:

- What is the cost of changing course at this point?
- What is the projected ROI—and timeline to ROI—of your idea?

This Isn't a Priority Right Now

Your stakeholders seem bought-in, but ultimately they defer their idea: "This sounds good—let's circle back in Q3," or "We're just too focused on [rebrand, product launch, reorg, fill-in-the-chaos] right now."

This is an indefinite delay, and it's worse than rejection. Often a vague response means they don't understand your strategy (see below), they think your strategy sucks, or sometimes it's that they simply don't like you and/or never wanted to hire you/your role in the first place but were pressured to by their board, exec team, stagnating sales, or some other external factor. Especially for content initiatives, which take more time to see results than execs are willing to wait and have non-linear impact on revenue.

When you get an indefinite delay (or even an outright no) response, don't argue and definitely don't share more details. Instead, sell them on the ways your strategy supports or integrates with the priorities they care about and can reduce costs and/or time to goal. Here are a few examples:

- How can your strategy increase the reach of the product launch and exponentially increase sign-ups throughout the quarter?

- For reorgs, in what ways will your content strategy positively impact internal sentiment to keep team productive? How might you use the reorg as a unique opportunity for brand awareness?

- If they are focused on sales-led growth, how will your strategy reduce demand, generate costs, and/or time-to-close?

I Don't Get It

"It" being your content marketing strategy. This is response you'll get from stakeholders the most, even when you've explained it using terms they understand and shown how it addresses the things they care about.

If your boss says, "I don't get it," then you still haven't the positioning right, and you need to lean further with curiosity to understand where they're coming from.

This will be infuriating at times, I know. But if your goal is to get your strategy approved, then getting curious is your way out.

Ok, ready for some tough love?

Here's a non-exhaustive list of things you might still be doing when pitching your strategy, even if you think you're not. I've made every one of these mistakes. In fact, the title of this section was inspired by a call I was on with a "big money guy" who said that exact phrase to me. Whoops!

- You're including too much detail
- You haven't crafted a logical argument with a narrative thread leading from big thing to results
- You're not presenting it with confidence so it comes across as confusing and when the CEO asks questions you don't give straight answers
- You're presenting ideas that are outside the CEO's marketing paradigm and you didn't accommodate for that in your presentation
- You didn't get buy-in from the stakeholders you needed to help translate

And here's a bonus reason precisely *zero* of you want to hear,

> Sometimes your content marketing strategy just isn't good.

There are countless reasons why creating a bad strategy is totally fine, especially if you don't take any of this too seriously. I mean, it's content marketing for *business-to-business companies*. There are no gurneys in sight and egos have a way of regenerating all on their own (for better or worse).

But the important reasons why it doesn't matter that you made a bad strategy are:

- You're the sort of person who is seeking education and improvement because you're reading a book about strategy (or your boss is making you read this, in which case I'm sorry, feel free to DM me for the Cliffs Notes, I got you).
- It's inevitable (remember?). Looking back, I pitched lots of bad ideas that, at the time, I thought were genius, and good for me, too! I learned a lot from confidently doing things wrong.

Conclusion

Much like marketing, the workplace reflects what it comprises: human beings with varying circumstances, beliefs, knowledge, and experiences. It changes constantly and often the same situation can't be solved the same way twice. The Answer to your challenges is rarely simple or binary, and it's almost never convenient or quick. Therefore, your actual job as a marketing leader isn't to create the best content marketing strategy; it is to create a strategy that will get *approved* then execute a strategy that will get results.

In my experience, some of the time you strategy works and sometimes it won't. Other times you'll do something by accident and it will be a huge success.

Whatever the circumstances, your chances of things "going to plan" are pretty much the same. There is a 50 percent chance things will "go to plan" and a 50 percent chance they won't. The most useful thing you can do is get as many reps in as possible, so you're less stressed when your plan doesn't work, or it does and it ends up being total chaos to execute so you actually wish you hadn't gotten buy-in for it in the first place.

Ultimately, the most helpful advice I can offer that applies to all circumstances you will encounter: You have to want to deal with the egos, business strategy, finance to get what you want and enjoy the process.

And by "want" I mean you need to be intrinsically motivated to navigate tricky workplace scenarios that involve surgeon-level emotional management at times if you want to get your way (no, you don't need to be a jerk) and most importantly, you must accept constant and never-ending change, because that's how companies work.

If you're in a marketing role with any sort of leadership expectation, even at small companies, there will be an inherent expectation from those around you that you will, well, manage.

Reporting, getting buy-in, managing all kinds of conflict, that's a big portion of your job in B2B marketing past manager level (though this role is not immune either) and it's not work that serves everyone. After all, burnout doesn't come from doing too much. It comes from doing work that doesn't serve you, in environments where you don't feel safe, seen, or in control of your own path.

"What would you like?" Cecilia Montalbano, my executive coach, asked me during our weekly sessions when I became CEO of Animalz.

We were in the middle of a pandemic, global cultural realities coming to bear, a rollercoaster of highs and lows in the B2B tech industry—you were there. And as a first-time CEO, I had no idea how to deal with any of it. Not to mention the surprising misogyny among the team, normal challenges that felt catastrophic because I'd never experienced them before, plus issues I created on my own.

My answer the whole time was always related to my role and the company. Most of the time, it was more like, "I want to do this better," or "I want to make this better." My personal mission as a leader: I wanted to prove that a company could produce objectively best-in-class work without being a jerk to the people who made it.

I chose to climb up on that pile of cow poo when I was nine. I asked for work I didn't know how to do so I could improve my skills. I didn't shy away from conflict. I chose to be accountable and, eventually, in charge.

And when it came to becoming a CEO, I didn't ask for it. I pointed at the founder and looked right in his eyes in a small room with the rest of the leadership team and said, "I want your job."

That was October 2019. By January 2020, I'd created a nine-month leadership transition plan that would culminate in a September announcement followed by three mini content "product" releases to reinforce our strength and dominance from the beginning of my leadership.

And as you all know, none of that went to plan.

Instead, we lost over $100k in MRR between February and March and foundational aspects of our lives were suddenly in flux, causing a chaos most of us had never encountered before.

And what only a few people know: The founder gave me an out. In a rare moment of compassion, he asked me if I still wanted to do it. The future wasn't looking great at the time, and I think he felt guilty about handing me the company under such challenging circumstances.

The question hadn't crossed my mind, and I was so caught off guard when he asked that I got angry. I even accused him of trying to convince me to change my mind because he didn't believe I could do the job (it was an emotional time!). He wasn't, of course, and once I calmed down, I said, "The team needs someone who can get them through this, and I'm the best equipped to do it. We need to make the transition now."

What I'm trying to say is that nothing ever went to plan. It hardly ever does. And if you accept that as part of the plan, you'll be more mentally prepared to handle unexpected things you encounter without getting so stressed. In some instances, you can even have fun.

But perhaps most importantly, regardless of what happens with anything you're doing, if your answer to "what would you like?" isn't the thing you're doing right now, go do something else.

Today, folks with marketing skills have more ways to make money than ever before. Many of the reasons you think you're stuck, you made up. They are not actual blockers:

- Your company will be perfectly fine, if not better, without you. Trust me.

- No, your reputation will not take a hit if you leave a company within two years or if you don't finish that project before you quit. Just leave.

- There will always be macro forces impacting jobs. Get into the micro and find the opportunity.

- You don't owe your company or your colleagues anything. Both would choose the opportunity over you.

And here's the thing: In the context of business, that's correct and totally fine. The CEO's *actual* job, it isn't to protect the people; it's to protect the business. That means, technically, the company doesn't have to do anything outside of whatever rules of governance they fall under. They are only incentivized to take care of you to the extent that it benefits them. Not everyone leads that way, but that's not the point either.

The point is that so long as it is this way and our world operates on this reality, you're better off accepting that reality without judgment first. Learn it, be open to understanding the parts that are ugly and how they came to be that way (it's usually something stupid, but still, it's good to know), participate in the parts that don't go against your values. Then find a way to make the institution work for you.

Or just leave.

I'm not telling you to "just deal" with unfairness. I'm telling you that the wind isn't the only force that can move you forward. Being the sun works too. And if you're lucky enough to have a choice, remember, when the sun shines bright, it melts ice into water and that water naturally flows down the mountain, into the river, and that river (well, most of them at least) keeps going until it meets the sea. It just takes a little longer.

INDEX

The main index is filed in alphabetical, word-by-word order. Acronyms and Mc are filed as presented; numbers are filed as spelt out. Locators in italics denote information within figures; those in roman numerals denote information within the foreword.

Looking for another book?

Explore our award-winning
books from global business
experts in Marketing and Sales

Scan the code to browse

www.koganpage.com/marketing

More from Kogan Page

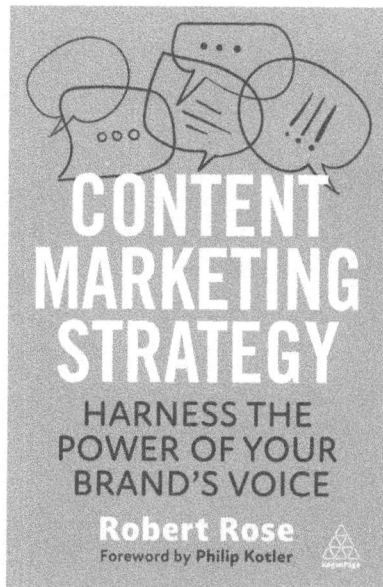

From 4 December 2025 the EU Responsible Person (GPSR) is:
eucomply oÜ, Pärnu mnt. 139b – 14, 11317 Tallinn, Estonia
www.eucompliancepartner.com

9 7 8 1 3 9 8 6 2 2 5 0 0